British packaging **NOW** · British packaging **NOW** · British packaging **NOW** · British packaging **NOW** · British packaging **NOW** · British packaging N

Edited by: *Edward Booth-Clibborn*

packaging **NOW** · British packaging **NOW** · British packaging **NOW** packaging **NOW** · British packaging **NOW** · British packaging **NOW** · Briti

Credits

Editor: *Edward Booth-Clibborn*

Assistant Editor: *Francis Glibbery*

Book Design: *Trickett & Webb Limited*

Cover Photography: *Jonathan Lovekin*

The captions and artwork in this book are based
on material supplied by the designers whose work
is included. While every effort has been made to
ensure their accuracy, "British Packaging Now"
does not under any circumstances accept any
responsibility for any errors or omissions.

*Printed and bound in Hong Kong
by Toppan Printing Co.*

*Published and distributed in the United
Kingdom. Direct mail rights in Europe
Internos Books Limited,
18 Colville Road,
London W3 8BL,
England*

ISBN No. 0904 866 998

*Distributors for the rest of the world:
Hearst Books International,
1350 Avenue of the Americas,
New York NY 10019,
United States of America*

*Distribution in the USA and Canada
rights reserved*

*Copyright © 1993
Booth-Clibborn Editions*

British packaging **NOW** • British packaging **NOW** • British pa

British packaging **NOW** •

Contents

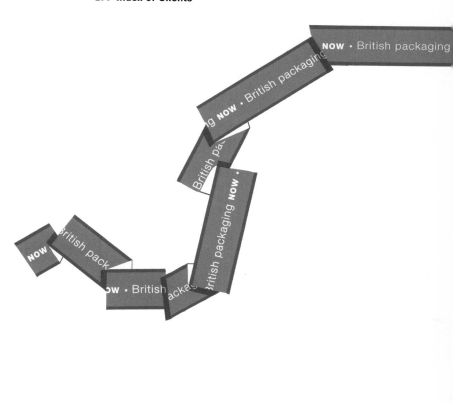

• British packaging **NOW** • British packaging **NOW** • British packaging **NOW** • British packaging **NOW** • British packaging **NOW** • British packaging **N**

Introduction

I n the five years since we published "The Best of British Packaging" I've been asked many times to produce a follow-up volume, to show how much packaging design has improved in Britain.

In the following pages you will see the work I have chosen as a celebration of the continuing excellence of British packaging design. All of it was commissioned by clients who clearly share my undying belief in the real value of high-quality creative thinking.

In every case, my criteria for including each item were simple. I judged each one only on the merits of its design and typography, the way the designers used illustration or photography, and each pack's ability to communicate valuable information about its contents in a visually interesting way.

For me, work which satisfies these essential requirements is always work which deserves celebration.

And it is work which always succeeds commercially, because it recognises that, no matter how much money has been spent on developing and perfecting any product, it will only sell well if it has been packaged well.

In the case-histories accompanying these examples you'll learn something of the creative and commercial problems involved in packaging design. Some of them hint at the complications of working with the sort of reduced budgets and technical constraints which could hinder lesser minds. They are all evidence of the ingenuity, invention and integrity which are now part and parcel of British packaging design.

If you are involved in packaging design as a professional, I hope this book will be an inspiration, as well as a mine of information.

If you are simply interested as a consumer, my hope is that next time you are out shopping you will ask yourself whether or not good design has helped you make your choices.

Edward Booth-Clibborn *1993*

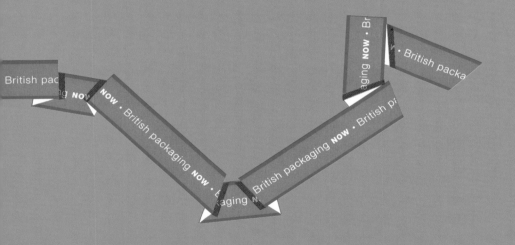

● Food Products

The products in this section include items such as breakfast cereals, complete meals, canned fruit and vegetables, soups, biscuits, cakes and bread, dairy products, teas, coffees and many others which can be found in supermarkets and specialist food shops all over Europe.

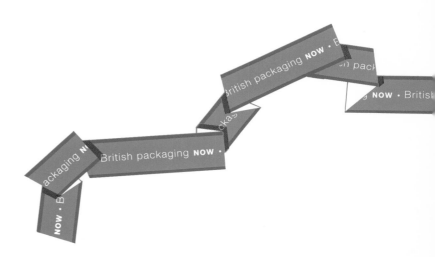

● *An own label range of cereals*
for William Low & Co plc
Designer: *Julie Catling*
Art Director: *Julie Catling*
Illustrator: *Iain McIntosh*

● **McIlroy Coates Limited**

McIlroy Coates' design uses illustration to explore the theme of morning sunshine for an own label range of breakfast cereals for the Scottish food group, William Low.

By varying the illustration, colour and typography, and by using descriptive copy as part of the image, each pack in the range - Crisp Rice, Breakfast Biscuits, Cornflakes and Bran Flakes - targets a specific group in the breakfast cereal market.

The branding device used to pull the range together and give it shelf impact is a flat colour panel containing the William Low logo and the individual product name. This is always placed to the right of the front face of each of the packs in the range.

● *Broadening the appeal of Tesco's*
Honey & Nut Cornflakes
Designer: *Kara Sims*
Art Director: *Chen Tsoi*
Illustrators: *Terry Hand*
and Richard Lewington
Photographer: *Paul Williams*

● Chen Tsoi Design

The previous design for Tesco's Honey & Nut Cornflakes featured a cartoon character which had been specifically designed to appeal to children.

The client felt that the new design should have a broader appeal and gave the designers an open brief to create a back-of-the-pack concept which would be readable at the breakfast table.

A playful combination of photography and typography has been used for the front of the pack, while the back has been designed in the style of a newspaper's front page offering information on bees and honey in an entertaining way.

The launch of the pack was very successful. Tesco's even received a letter from the Beekeepers Association, complimenting them on the accuracy of the information. A second version of this has since been introduced.

● *Tesco's new premium muesli*
Designer: *Robin Hall*
Art Director: *Robin Hall*
Illustrator: *Robin Hall*

● **Davies Hall**

Davies Hall were briefed by Tesco Stores to design the packaging for their two new premium breakfast cereals for the adult market. The new-style muesli has a base of toasted oats which gives it a crunchy quality and a fuller taste.

Botanical style illustrations emphasise the product's natural high quality ingredients. The crunchy nature of the product is stressed in its title and reiterated in the hand-drawn lettering of the word "crunchy" running down the centre of the pack.

The result is a premium presentation which stresses the three main product attributes: taste, crunchiness and quality.

● A break with tradition
for the Co-op's cereal range
Designer: *Elaine Morgan*
Art Director: *Elaine Morgan*
Photographer: *Laurence Hudghton*
Illustrator: *Anthea Helliwell*

● Co-operative Wholesale Society Limited

In recent years it has become much more socially acceptable to admit to eating breakfast cereals, and not just at breakfast time. They are even appearing on the menus of fashionable snack and cafe bars.

With this in mind, when the Co-op decided to up-date their existing cereal range, they also wanted to be able to introduce some unusual new products of their own, such as Choc & Nut Cornflakes.

But to try to compete with a look-alike pack design usually leads consumers to expect an inferior product. So it was decided to produce an "any time of the day" design; one which did not focus on the limiting images of mornings or breakfast time.

The interesting overhead shot of the bowl, surrounded by lots of its ingredients, is deftly used in conjunction with the main feature of the design: a unique wood-cut-style illustration running down the left-hand side of the pack in a torn strip which enhances the "rustic" quality of the overall image.

As colour is always an important identifier for consumers, all the packs have strong colour coding which helps with their impact on the shelf.

● *A new range of exotic ready*
meals for Sainsbury's
Designer: *Steve Davies*
Art Director: *Steve Davies*
Photographer: *Paul Kemp*

● **Davies Hall**

Sainsbury's range of Marinated Chicken ready meals consists of four chicken dishes in exotic marinades.

Davies Hall's combination of strong background colours and appetising photographs both differentiate the products and hint at the origins of the recipes. The photographs of the meals beside the ingredients of their marinades give the packs an exotic appeal. The white flavour trail and back panel create a strong and cohesive identity for the range.

● *Targeting the busy woman for*
The Boots Company
Designer: *Lucilla Scrimgeour*
Art Director: *Mary Lewis*
Photographer: *Jess Koppel*

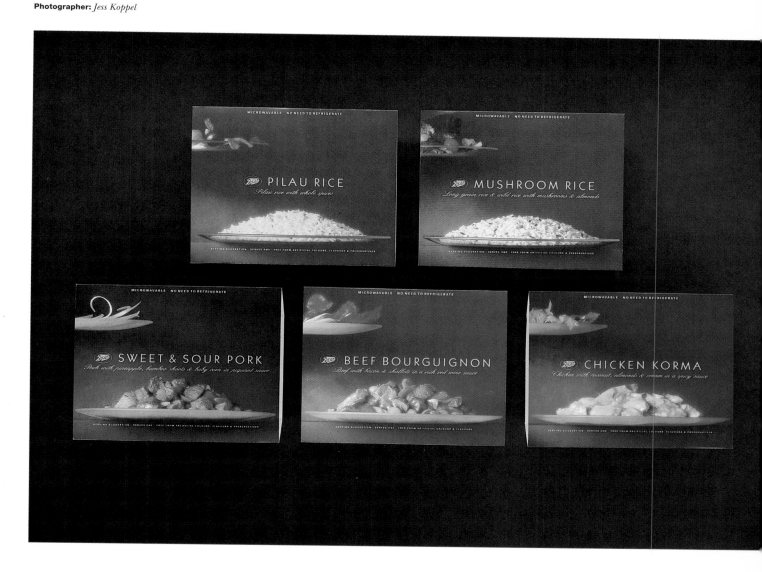

● **Lewis Moberly**

Created for the busy working woman who shops in her lunch hour, Boots Evening Meals are premium products designed for the microwave.

The packaging designers' brief was to create simple, strong, appetising imagery with the minimum of information communicated at the right level.

The design focuses on the product itself, reassuring the consumer of its quality through photographs taken against rich, coded backgrounds.

Minale, Tattersfield & Partners

Tesco's main objective in their brief to Minale Tattersfield was to enhance the company's leading position in the booming retail marketplace.

Their range of ready meals runs to a total of over fifty packs, each of which had to carry a corporate style and a product description.

The solution to the problem is a coloured panel which always holds the product title and is over-printed by its own seal together with a mouthwatering photograph of each particular meal.

The overall design reflects the new, healthy approach to pre-prepared meals.

● *Tesco's ready meals range*
Designer: *Ian Delaney*
Art Director: *Ian Delaney*

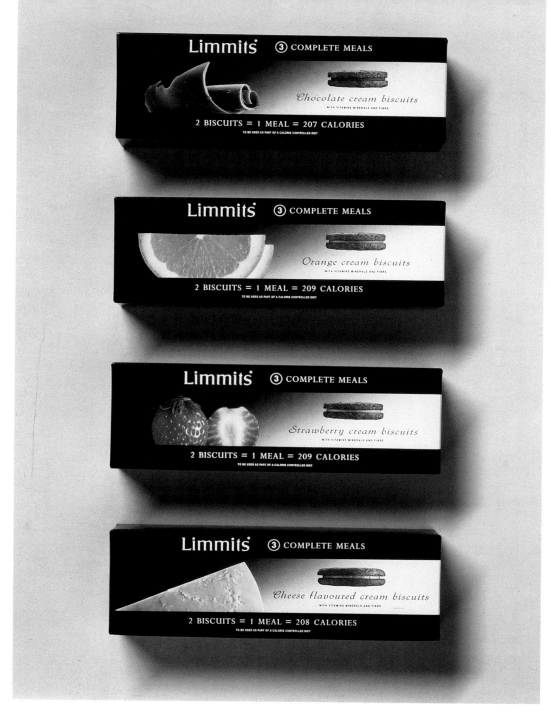

Lewis Moberly

Limmits are complete meals for slimmers, sold into a market which typically adopts wishy washy packs complete with tape measure graphics signalling "you are on a diet". The products often look unappetising, have little "eat me" appeal and bombard consumers with a barrage of information which they are expected to digest.

The number of calories each biscuit contains and how many to eat is obviously important. In this design the products are projected as being light and delicious, with their key ingredients photographed in such a way as to create plenty of appetite appeal.

Moreover, the key information about the calorific contents of the pack is communicated in a simple, direct way, making it easy to read at the point of sale.

"Eat me" appeal for Scholl
Consumer Products
Designers: *Jimmy Yang
and Mary Lewis*
Art Director: *Mary Lewis*
Photographer: *Robin Broadbent*

Nettle Design Limited

The canned soup business, which is split into standard, low calorie and premium sectors, is one of the largest divisions of the grocery market.

Asda's brief to Nettle Design was for a design concept for their Speciality Soup range; one which would convey an image of top quality products specially produced for special occasions.

The Asda logo is smaller than on the store's usual commodity lines, which helps to convey an image of sophistication. This is augmented by the use of a black panel in which the type is featured over a photo-graph of a celebratory meal, thus positioning the products at the premium end of the market.

● *Special designs for special soups from Asda Stores*
Designer: *Glyn West*
Art Director: *Glyn West*
Photographer: *Alan Marsh*

• *Fish finger serving suggestions*
  for Safeway Stores plc
  Designer: *Ray Kyte*
  Art Director: *Ray Kyte*
  Photographer: *Adam Tolner*

• Kyte & Company Limited

Safeway commissioned Kyte & Company to produce designs for three grades of fish fingers: a basic economy pack (which had to fit in with a generic styling already established by Kyte & Company for a wide range of economy products), a standard pack and the premium fillet fish fingers featured here.

The brief called for a pack design which included a serving suggestion.

Ray Kyte chose to photograph the product outside a place setting, in a rich, moody and dramatic manner, with the product dominant in the design and displaying all the quality within its breadcrumb coating.

The packs' fresh, clean appearance was created through the use of simple, elegant typography.

Trickett & Webb Limited

T rickett & Webb's original
brief from Tesco was for a
design scheme which would differentiate their various grades of
fresh fruit and vegetables and
prepared salads.

Part of the problem was the need
for a style which could be repro-
duced by several different printers
working for a wide variety of suppliers, all of whom would be expected to meet Tesco's high standards
of presentation.

The solution is an almost minimalist design. Celebrating the
freshness of each product, it trans-
forms each item into a work of art
by Glynn Boyd-Harte, an illustrator
noted for his light and delicate
touch.

In some cases the fruits and vegetables are shown sliced open, to
give the consumer a glimpse of
their inner quality. In every case
the design allows for a short
description of the product and
includes boxes for the price and
sell by date and a checkout bar
code.

The second stage of the project
involved the production of a
design manual for printers to help
them produce new labels at short
notice, to allow for new lines as
they were introduced. In the later
stages of the project, designs were
also supplied for added value
flashes with messages such as
"Extra Fresh By Air".

● *Fresh designs for fresh foods
from Tesco Stores*
Designers: *Sarah Mattinson,
Lynn Trickett and Brian Webb*
Art Directors: *Lynn Trickett
and Brian Webb*
Illustrator: *Glynn Boyd-Harte*

● *Packaging innovation for*
  Safeway Stores
  Designer: *Kathy Miller*
  Art Director: *Glenn Tutssel*
  Photographer: *David Gill*

● **Michael Peters Limited**

This piece of packaging design is part of a huge corporate and brand identity programme being carried out for Safeway Stores.

The innovative graphics show the can "peeled back" to reveal its contents.

Nettle Design Limited

In recent years the canned vegetable market has been in decline as consumers' preferences have moved more and more towards frozen vegetables and supermarkets sell more fresh produce.

Against this background, Asda identified a market for a range of premium canned vegetables, either as single varieties or as combinations such as Garden Peas and Sweetcorn.

Nettle Design were briefed to create new packaging which would reflect the quality and freshness of the products, and give the cans a strong identity on the supermarket shelf.

A new look for Asda's range of canned vegetables
Designer: *Glyn West*
Art Director: *Glyn West*
Illustrator: *Peter Ross*

● *Colour coded frozen vegetables*
for Safeway Stores plc
Designers/Art Directors: *Ray Kyte*
and Andrew Sutton
Photographers: *Adam Tolner*
and Christine Hanscombe

● **Kyte & Company**

Safeways commissioned Kyte &
Company to design packaging
for their entire range of Standard
and Premium frozen vegetables.
  With so many varieties of vegetables
in the freezer cabinets, Kyte &
Company decided to create a clean,
simple and direct design style, using
colour-coded backgrounds and photographs to show the shape of the
vegetables and help customers
recognise each product.

● *New Soy Sauces for Lea & Perrins*
Designer: *Christine Simmons*
Art Director: *Roger Bannister*

● **Springett Associates**

Asked to develop a new range of Soy Sauces, Springett Associates were already familiar with the Lea & Perrins brand, having developed the identity for the company's famous flagship brand, Worcestershire Sauce.

This time Lea & Perrins wanted to introduce a new range of Soy Sauces with a difference, capitalising on their expertise as blenders of unique flavours. An in-depth understanding

of the difference between corporate, brand and product identities and the role each can play in structuring and growing product portfolios was vital in this project.

The result is a range of four different Soy Sauces, sold in the traditional Lea & Perrins bottle but with a wholly contemporary look. Vertical bands of vibrant colour and typography on the labels and brightly coloured lids evoke the flavour of the sauces inside, with a distinct Chinese emphasis. The Lea & Perrins brand

name is emphasised in a strong band across the label top, and reinforced with the well-known signature on the side. The new range has been designed to achieve high visibility on the shelf as an exciting new product from Lea & Perrins.

On the bottle label:

SAINSBURY'S

S·P·A·N·I·S·H
SHERRY
VINEGAR

MADE FROM
FINO SHERRY

FOR SALAD DRESSINGS, SAUCES
& MARINADES

This fine quality Sherry
Vinegar is matured for
several years in old
Sherry casks using the
traditional Solera method.

ONCE OPENED STORE IN A COOL DRY PLACE

Produced by JOSE PEMARTIN, JEREZ DE LA FRONTERA, SPAIN

350 ml ℮

The Team

This Spanish sherry vinegar was launched as the premium product in Sainsbury's own range of speciality vinegars.

The brief was to position it as a product superior to other major brands and own-label equivalents.

The traditional sherry bottle was seen as being intrinsic in presenting the authenticity and method of producing the vinegar. The collaged illustration reflects the product's Spanish heritage and its refined, delicate flavour.

● *Sainsbury's superior Spanish sherry vinegar*
Designer: *Yasmin Betteridge*
Art Director: *Richard Ward*
Illustrator: *David Loftus*

The Team

This own-label, premium quality vinegar was launched as a speciality product, targeted at the adventurous consumer looking for an alternative to wine vinegar.

It was vital that the design reflected the product's authentic Italian origins in Modena. A gold stock was chosen for the label to portray the character of the vinegar and set off the label against the rich, dark colour of the product itself. The etched illustrations of barrels and grapes give a subtle indication of the method of production: grape juice which is concentrated over a low flame and then mellowed and aged for a lengthy period in barrels of various woods.

Projecting the Italian origins of Sainsbury's Balsamic Vinegar
Designers: *Nicole Clément-Weiss and Richard Ward*
Art Director: *Richard Ward*

Southern American designs for
Discovery Foods
Designer: *Glyn West*
Art Director: *Glyn West*
Illustrator: *Peter Ross*

● **Nettle Design Limited**

Discovery Foods is a small
family-owned company
specialising in Mexican and South
Western American foods which
were launched in 1989 to cater for
the increasing popularity of this
style of cooking.

Although the products originally
enjoyed considerable approval
amongst consumers, the packaging
was seen as being weak and with
limited appeal.

Nettle Design's new packaging
combines ethnic and traditional
styles of illustration and typography, giving a more distinctive
and authentic look to the range
than some of the "anglicised"
competition.

Since the re-launch, sales have
increased by over 50% in certain
supermarkets and many new
orders have been placed with
the client.

Horseman Cooke

A desire for strong branding, colour coding, clear product descriptions and photography are all part of a Somerfield brief.

The company's Gravy Granules range required a touch of nostalgia, but without the drawbacks of an out-and-out pastiche.

The label device uses a simple graphic illustration and hand drawn type. When the pack is tilted, the label creates an illusionary integration of the pouring gravy and the photographic image of a serving suggestion.

Gateway's Somerfield
Gravy Granules
Designer: *Gary Cooke*
Art Directors: *Gary Cooke*
and Laverne Bailey
Photographer: *Struan Wallace*
Illustrators: *Mouseworks*

● Greenwich Design Associates

The Victorian values of an "Upstairs Downstairs" style of good, honest home cooking were those which Marks & Spencer and Greenwich Design Associates decided were right for the re-design of a range of gravy granule packs.

The strong colours and unique border patterns of the new design allow for the possible extension of the product range. The hand-drawn typefaces, influenced by a study of Victorian packaging, are designed to bring the right values to an already established product which is being marketed in a new and more convenient form.

Shelf impact for the new line was an important consideration throughout the project, as was the fact that the designs were to be translated to trays. These and the packs had to succeed in balancing the needs of a modern supermarket environment with a sense of traditional authenticity and quality.

*Designs which hint at flavours
for Safeway's tinned meats
Designers: Steve Edwards,
Lynn Trickett and Brian Webb
Art Directors: Lynn Trickett
and Brian Webb*

● **Trickett & Webb Limited**

The key element in Safeway's
brief for their selection of
tinned meats was that the name of
each product should be clearly and
quickly understood in the store.

The range includes Irish Stew, Chili
con Carne, Corned Beef,
Frankfurters and a variety of Curries.

Trickett & Webb's simple solution
to the problem was to photograph
each product on a suitably atmospheric background - a scrubbed

wooden table top for Irish Stew and
a baked clay background for the chili,
for example - and surround each
image with strong typography.

The design also allows the tins to be
stacked on the shelf in such a way as
to form a continuous pattern.

These products are good examples
of Safeway's determination to give all
their own label lines a strong brand
identity which will compete well in
the store.

● *Safeway's range of exotic fruits*
Designer: *Barry Gillibrand*
Art Director: *Barry Gillibrand*
Photographer: *Jess Koppel*

● **Davies Hall**

The Safeway's range of exotic fruits features canned fruits from Thailand.

Photographed by Jess Koppel, the fruits are treated like jewels against vibrant hand-painted backgrounds.

To further create an impression of quality, Davies Hall contrasted strong pack colours with delicate traditional-style patterns which echo the exotic oriental origins of the fruits.

● *Simplifying the shoppers' choice
for Waitrose's canned fruits*
Designers: *Karin Dunbar,
Mary Lewis and Ann Marshall*
Art Director: *Mary Lewis*
Illustrators: *Karin Dunbar
and Joanne Smith*

● **Lewis Moberly**

Waitrose has for many years had an enviable reputation for the high quality of its own label products. In this particular sector there are many different canned fruits. Each fruit has several varieties of form, each prepared in either syrup or fruit juice. It's distinctions like these which have to be made clear for consumers. The design solution aims to simplify the selection process by using symbolic fruit images which clearly describe the form, and by coding the distinctions between fruit and syrup juices in a focused panel of colour against a cohesive dark green background.

● *Colourful fruit salad packs for*
Tesco Stores Limited
Designer: *Ray Kyte*
Art Director: *Ray Kyte*
Illustrator: *Jeremy Sancha*

● Kyte & Company Limited

Tesco's fruit salad is packed in oval, see-through plastic trays with card sleeves.

Kyte & Company wanted to contrast the colours of the fruit salad with a strong design which would clearly indicate the selection of fruits in each pack. A black background was chosen to give a neutral setting against which the illustration could really punch out the colours in the fruit.

Interestingly, black is rarely used in food packaging, other than for type.

● *Bold colours and classic*
typography for Gruppo Rinascente
Designer: *Nick Hanson*
Art Director: *Glenn Tutssel*
Photographer: *David Gill*

● Michael Peters Limited

This range of canned fruits from Gruppo Rinascente draws its strong visual identity from a combination of bold background colours, classic typography and an interesting image of each can's contents.

The overall effect is a reflection of the client's reputation as a retailer of high quality own label products.

● *A Greek theme for*
Waitrose's yoghurt design
Designers: *Graham Purnell*
and Ian Prevett
Art Director: *Brian Delaney*
Illustrator: *Christine Simpson*

● **Delaney Design Consultants**

Waitrose's brief for this project called for a design which would present the yoghurt as a clean, refreshing product.

Once in the stores, the packs are seen primarily from above. There are four flavours in the range, and particular attention had to be paid to the differing qualities of the packaging materials being used.

The solution features a Greek column as a plinth, with each different flavour placed on top. There are also colour variations within the columns.

Once this theme had been established, the next problem was to find an illustrative style suitable for the different printing methods being used for the pot and the lid. The plastic pot is printed flexo, so a simple lino cut style was chosen.

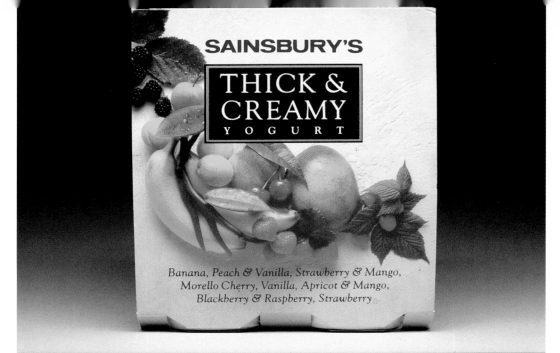

Davies Hall

Sainsbury's market several yoghurt ranges. Thick & Creamy Yoghurts are their premium products.

Davies Hall decided on a photographic approach for these designs, to maximise the feel of a quality product and differentiate these yoghurts from the many others which use illustration as part of their approach.

A soft plaster wall acts as a backdrop for the fruits and suggests the creaminess of the yoghurt. The beautiful photographs of lush, ripe fruits - complete with their leaves - convey the idea that the yoghurts are packed full of freshly picked fruit. The multi-pack sleeve features a sumptuous still life of mixed fruits.

The elegant black panel gives prominence to the brand name and further enhances the image of quality and indulgence.

Sainsbury's Thick and Creamy Yoghurts
Designer: Barry Gillibrand
Art Director: Barry Gillibrand
Photographer: Jess Koppel

A wickedly simple idea
for Chambourcy
Designers: *Elaine Craig,*
Lynn Trickett and Brian Webb
Art Directors: *Lynn Trickett*
and Brian Webb

Trickett & Webb Limited

With a name like Chocoholics, Chambourcy's rich dessert is clearly not designed for weight-watchers. Its recipe includes a mixture of milk, white and plain chocolate in three layers, topped off with cream.

Trickett & Webb's witty design for the product's cardboard sleeve - with its amusing horns and devilish tail - acknowledges the recipe's luscious qualities, and positions Chocoholics as wicked without being sinful.

As an example of story-telling packaging, it offers endless creative possibilities for advertising and promotional activities.

● Delaney Design Consultants

These chocolate and lemon flavoured mousses are part of a range of desserts offered by Waitrose.

The packaging brief called for a design which would emphasise the luxurious quality of the products, and make them stand out in an area where there is heavy competition from branded goods.

The designers' solution was to feature the main flavouring of each product by photographing each one in atmospheric lighting on a textured paper background. The lighting changes colour on each pack in sympathy with each flavour, thus creating a natural distinction between each product in the range.

Colourful designs for Waitrose
Fruit Fools
Designers: *Graham Purnell
and Jeff Willis*
Art Director: *Brian Delaney*
Photographer: *Andy Seymour*

Delaney Design Consultants

The brief for these fruit fools called for a strong, uncluttered, colourful design which would establish the products as luxury items in an area subject to considerable competition from branded goods.

The designers also had to overcome the problems posed by a predominately white product being sold from a white cabinet.

As with the designs for Waitrose Mousses, the solution features the main flavouring of each product through the use of atmospheric lighting and textured paper backgrounds. The strong individual colours of each flavour give each pack a natural distinction within the range.

● *New English designs for cheeses*
from Tesco Stores Limited
Designer: *Ray Kyte*
Illustrator: *Ray Kyte*

● Kyte & Company Limited

Kyte & Company's brief from Tesco was to create a new style of lively, informative designs for a wide variety of English cheese labels, including territorials, economy lines, regional cheddars and the "cut from the round" traditional cheeses shown here.

TESCO

SAVOURY

BISCUITS FOR CHEESE

VARIETIES OF BISCUITS FOR CHEESE IN A
HANDY PRESENTATION TRAY (SEE BACK OF PACK)
5

200 g ℮

● *Reflections of quality for*
Tesco's cheese biscuits
Designers/Art Directors:
Mike Staniford and Ray Betts
Photographer: *Paul Kemp*

● **Hutton Staniford**

Hutton Staniford's brief was to create an all-year-round design for Tesco's biscuits for cheese which would emphasise the quality and range of the different biscuit varieties.

The design had to be photographic and full colour, and work within the constraints of a predetermined box shape.

The style of photography and choice of typography reinforce the concept of a high quality product.

● *A traditional image for Katsouris*
Brothers' taramosalata
Designer: *Philip Carter*
Art Director: *Philip Carter*
Illustrator: *Andrew Davidson*

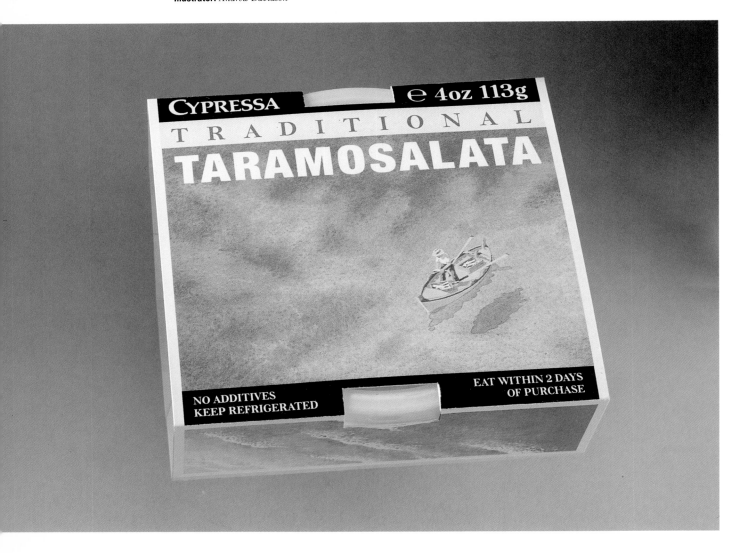

● Carter Wong

Katsouris Brothers Limited, importers of authentic Greek produce, have been clients of Carter Wong's for some years.

In this instance, their brief to the designers was to convey the fact that their taramosalata was an original product, and thus give it an edge over the competition.

Carter Wong commissioned an illustrator to create an image of the taramosalata's origins through the portrayal of most consumers' idea of a traditional Greek fishing scene.

The new packaging has added to the product's image of authenticity, and sales and distribution have both increased.

● *A family feel for Galbani's*
famous cheeses
Designers: *Ian Grindle*
and Liz Knight
Art Director: *Marcello Minale*
Illustrator: *Yvonne Watson*

● **Minale, Tattersfield & Partners**

As the major cheese producer in the Italian market, Galbani commissioned Minale Tattersfield to reappraise the packaging of its Mozzarella, Dolcelatte, Mascarpone, Magor, Ricotta and Parmesan cheeses.

Following a Europe-wide audit, the designers developed packaging with a strong family feel which retains some of the earlier elements - such as the gingham pattern - and introduces an Italian landscape image which evokes the products' heritage.

Serving suggestions are also part of the design, to help customers who are less familiar with the origins of these cheeses and how the individual types can be used in everyday cooking.

In each case, the copy on the pack appears in the language of the country in which the products are sold.

● *Successful designs for Busha Browne's*
Jamaican preserves
Designer: *Michael Thierens*
Art Director: *Michael Thierens*
Illustrator: *Ian Beck*

● **Michael Thierens Design**

Busha Browne's Company of Jamaica produce a range of natural preserves and sauces made to 19th century Jamaican recipes dating from the days of the British plantocracy and aimed primarily at American markets both as tourist gifts bought in Jamaica and for export to top American food stores.

The sophistication of the outlets called for a subtle on-shelf strength as well as an understated visual appeal. The packaging also had to be suitable for a wide variety of jars and cartons.

Each product label uses hand-drawn typography inspired by Jamaican wood carvings. The muted earth tones create lush tropical associations with the natural products and avoid the stridency of primary colours so often employed in a Caribbean context.

The range is highly successful, enjoying a position at the forefront of the USA gourmet food market where it is regarded as most individual.

● *Design that stands out for*
Co-op Brand's ethnic range
Designer: *Jasbinder Singh*
Art Director: *Jasbinder Singh*
Photographer: *Laurence Hudghton*
Illustrators: *The Northern Art Collection*

● Co-operative Wholesale Society Limited

The market for ethnic foods and ingredients for interesting meals has grown rapidly over the last five years, as more people travel abroad and the number of good restaurants and take-aways at home increases.

The design brief for the Co-op's range for this market called for an authentic, high quality, bright and strong series of sleeved packs which would have in-store cabinet presence, consumer appeal and be able to stand out from the competition.

With impact in mind, the designer decided to use a powerful overall background image, scanned with commissioned illustrations and combined graphics on the Apple Mac. This was first constructed at low resolution and then manipulated in photoshop. Quark Xpress was used to create final design concepts for presentation to the client; it was then simple to extend the approved concept to the entire range, again using the computer.

The range of products includes Onion Bhajis, Vegetable Spring Rolls, and Vegetable and Meat Samosas.

● *Luxury liqueur preserves for*
Crabtree & Evelyn
Designer: *Penelope Parker*
Art Director: *Peter Windett*
Illustrator: *Karen Murray*

● **Peter Windett & Associates**

This brief was definite in its specific call for a rich, warm image for a range of luxury liqueur jams which would be distinguishable from the client's existing ranges of high quality preserves.

The illustrator, Karen Murray, was asked to focus on the raw fruit ingredients of the jams at harvest. Painted in oils, these essentially simple still life images have a great sumptuousness and richness of colour which is underpinned by the choice of a classic dark green for the panel and the use of gold for the type.

*Classic typography for the
English Provender Company*
Designer: *Julia White*
Art Director: *Julia White*

● Elmwood Design Limited

The English Provender
Company - manufacturers of
fine preserves for the gift market
and exclusive retail outlets -
commissioned Elmwood Design to
re-package their existing range of
preserves, condiments, vinegars and
flower waters.

The designer created a classical
typographic solution as an alternative
to the rustic themes so widely used
on many similar products.

A new company seal was devised
to complement the label design,
and this is repeated in relief on the
sides of the preserve jars.

The company name, English
Provender (originally a provider of
hay or fodder), is echoed in the
promise "Providers of fine quality
preserves" which appears in a
roundel device on each label.

Lewis Moberly

This packaging for Safeway Shortbread is designed to project the premium quality of the product.

Conventional typography has been avoided by embroidering the name of each biscuit variety onto a label stitched onto a traditional tartan rug.

The design reflects the Scottish origins of the biscuits and conjures up images of an enjoyable picnic.

• *Exploiting a Scottish tradition*
  for Safeway plc
  Designer: *Bruce Duckworth*
  Art Director: *Mary Lewis*
  Photographer: *Laurie Evans*

● *High quality shortbread from Tesco*

Designers/Art Directors:
Mike Staniford and Ray Betts
Photographer: *Paul Kemp*
Illustrator: *Wolf Spoerl*

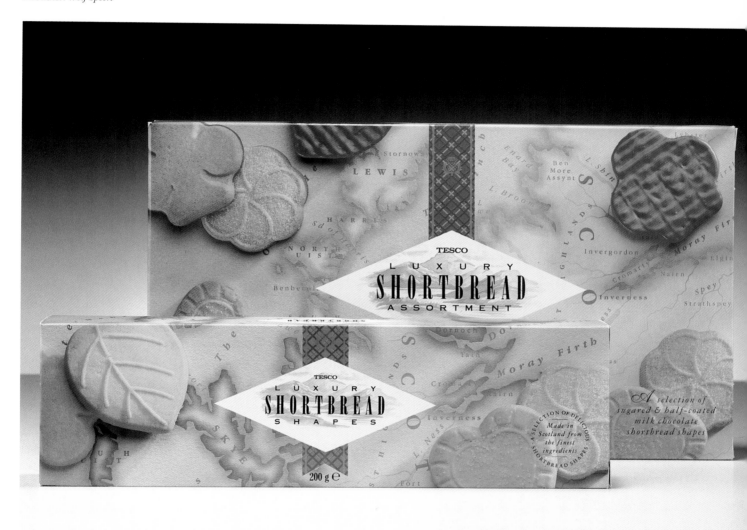

● Hutton Staniford

Hutton Staniford's brief from Tesco was to design the packaging for a range of high quality shortbread biscuits, investing them with a strong traditional Scottish feel.

One of the major selling points for the product is the interesting shapes they are baked in.

The designers decided to photograph the biscuits on specially commissioned maps of Scotland, to create a sense of their origins and authenticity. Bought-in maps proved to be too busy, with too much information and too little colour. By changing the base colours in the maps each time, the designers were also able to create a colour coding system for the entire range of biscuits involved.

The design solution combines the rich photography with clear and simple typography, set in a panel to suggest an applied label, thus enhancing the overall quality of the product.

*Exotically flavoured biscuits
for Crabtree & Evelyn*
Designer: *Wendy Gardiner*
Art Director: *Peter Windett*
Illustrator: *Tony McSweeney*

● Peter Windett & Associates

The need for this new range of exotically flavoured biscuits was for packaging which would be distinctive and yet not conflict with the traditional, well-established look of Crabtree & Evelyn's other products.

The idea emerged in discussion of using a tree as a central feature in each illustration on the tins. Not only would the trees indicate the respective flavours of the biscuits, but

they would also form a subtle link between these new products and the crabapple tree adopted by Crabtree & Evelyn as their logo. The illustrations themselves are of scenes drawn from the countries where the flavourings come from. In their fine delicate style, they have some of the qualities seen in Victorian lithographic images of colonial times.

With their warm and bold colours, the tins make a strong statement on the shop shelf. While the panels on the labels are elaborate and formal,

these characteristics are balanced by the movement in the distinguishing, punchy typefaces.

● *Seasonal cheer for J Sainsbury plc*
Designer: *Tessa Denison*
Art Director: *Annie Thomas*
Illustrator: *Steve Pearse*

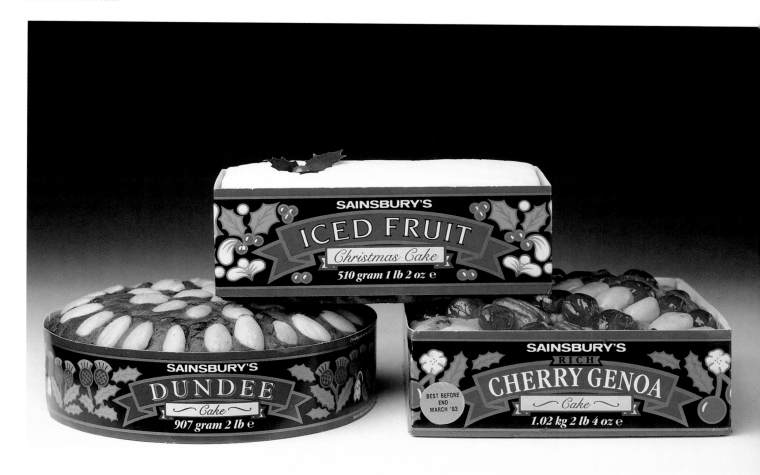

● Denison Thomas

Denison Thomas were briefed to design the packaging for a range of Sainsbury's Christmas Cakes which would be sold alongside the company's boxed cakes.

With only a wraparound paper label to work with, the designers needed to produce a bold and colourful image so that the cakes would stand out on the shelf without losing anything which spoke of their fine quality.

The solution employs a black background and gold imagery across the entire range, coupled with illustrations for each band which use the fruits and traditional foliage of the Christmas season.

The resulting design creates strong shelf impact, without detracting from the decorative surface of the cake.

Miller Sutherland

The Innes family are producers of England's premier fromage de chêvre and traditional sour-dough bread.

Their speciality foods are made with the finest organic ingredients, using traditional methods of production. The sour-dough bread, for example, takes six days to rise before it is baked in a 200-year-old wood-fired stone oven brought over to England from the South of France.

Miller Sutherland's brief for this project was to create an identity, packaging and promotional material which would reflect the Innes family's uncompromising dedication to their work, and provide a solid base for their expansion into national retail outlets.

The new identity uses elements of the family crest to capitalise on the quality and authority of the Innes heritage.

● *Reflecting traditional values for the Innes family's foods*
Designer: *Kathy Miller*
Art Director: *Kathy Miller*

● *A new identity for*
Roberts Bakery of Northwich
Designers/Art Directors:
Melvyn Harleyand Satish Lada

● **Chambers & Harley**

Roberts Bakery of Northwich commissioned Chambers & Harley to re-design their corporate identity which, once it had been approved, necessitated bringing their range of sliced bread, including the wholemeal range, into the new scheme of things.

   The packaging, which colour codes the variations of thick and medium slices, relies on a largely see-through solution to depict Roberts' quality and traditional product proposition in a modern yet classic way.

The Team

The brief for the re-design of Tesco's Wholenut Peanut Butter embraced every aspect of the packaging, from a new jar shape through to a new, tamper-proof label.

In terms of the product's personality, the objective was to give it a more up-market image than before, and portray it as a natural, healthy alternative to the other, unskinned varieties on the market.

● *A more up-market image for Tesco's peanut butter*
Designer: *Yasmin Betteridge*
Art Director: *Richard Ward*
Illustrator: *Yasmin Betteridge*

Chocolate biscuits for
Christmas from Jacobs
Designer: *Nick Hanson*
Art Director: *Glenn Tutssel*
Illustrator: *Graham Evernden*

● Michael Peters Limited

The design of this novelty tin of biscuits sets out to recapture the spirit of Christmas past.

The embossed tin structure is designed as a ceremonial drum, complete with drumsticks and a silk shoulder cord.

The surface graphics include seven intricate crests, each displaying a partly hidden chocolate biscuit and a uniformed character playing a musical instrument.

The nostalgic qualities of the design help to create a product which has its own endearing charm.

● *Generic packaging for*
The Farmers Dairy Company
Designer: *Vince Frost*
Art Director: *John Rushworth*
Photographer: *Steve Rees*

● **Pentagram Design Limited**

The Farmers Dairy Company is a group of small, independent organic dairy farmers competing with larger dairy producers in the major supermarket chains.

In addition to a new identity for the co-operative, Pentagram was commissioned to develop generic packaging for a range of dairy products, including different milks and yoghurts, which would compete with other supermarket brands.

Strong, simple typography creates a brand identity, while a simple, quiet photograph of a wild grass, fruit or flower conveys an image of nature's goodness. The name of the producing farm acts as a sub-brand.

As the product range is extended, new packaging is developed, paid for centrally by the co-operative.

The identity and packaging system give each producer the economic benefits of scale without depriving the consumer of the attraction of locally produced, farm-fresh products. For the retailer, there is the added benefit of a convenient nationwide network of suppliers.

USE BY

e 500 ml

milk
Bio

EXPRESS

Bio Bio

WITH NATURAL · B.A. CULTURES

FRESH PASTEURISED
SEMI-SKIMMED

● *Express Dairy's Bio milk*
Designer: *David Spencer*
Art Director: *David Spencer*

● **David Spencer Design
Partnership**

E xpress Dairies called in the
David Spencer Design Partnership to help them launch a number
of new products destined for the
chilled cabinet sector of the retail
market.

One of these products was Bio, a
milk with natural cultures which
benefit digestion.

The brief called for a distinctive
design which would convey the
natural, healthy up-to-the-minute
qualities of the product.

The problem of how to create
strong shelf stand out without
resorting to the clichés usually
used in the dairy sector was solved
by employing a clean, crisp,
modern design which has no dairy
images at all.

● *White milk in cartons for
Safeway Stores plc*
Designer: *Ray Kyte*
Art Director: *Ray Kyte*
Illustrator: *Clifford Harper*

● Kyte & Company Limited

Kyte & Company had long held the belief that milk should be presented in primarily white cartons. We are all very familiar with the whiteness of milk in bottles, yet no-one had dealt with this before Ray Kyte got the Safeway brief.

His first consideration was to use a lot of white space and to use colour very sparingly, simply to code the various types of milk.

The brief specifically vetoed the depiction of cows, and also included restrictions created by the printing process involved. This had an important influence on the general direction of the design thinking.

A country feel was created through the use of imitation woodcuts of farming scenes which, because of their technique, were also ideally suited to the flexo printing method.

*A new image for teas from
Tesco Stores Limited*
Designer: *Jonathan Humphrey*
Art Director: *Patricia Shiel*
Illustrators: *Moira Chesmur
and Caroline Church*

● Shiel Humphrey Design

This range of speciality tea packs was commissioned by Tesco as part of a complete re-design of their entire range of teas.

The company's complete range was first sub-divided into various groups, including speciality teas and tea bags. Tesco asked Shiel Humphrey to create a theme which could be used across the full range, but which would also allow each pack to be treated individually.

The solution to this part of the problem was the tea leaf logo in its diamond, which has been used with the Tesco logo as a branding device on all the packs. This gives the entire range a quality image, and allows the designers to work on each pack in an individual way.

Considerable research was carried out on the origins and style of each tea, and on sources for the final watercolour illustrations. Each pack was colour coded to denote the various countries of origin, and to make

it easier for repeat purchase customers to identify their favourite type of tea. The illustrations' subject matter, together with the tea logos, combine to create a family feel for the entire range of teas.

The main illustrations were briefed out to Moira Chesmur, with tight guidelines based on Shiel Humphrey's original work, while the tea leaf illustrations were briefed separately to Caroline Church.

Springett Associates

Twinings' strength in the herbal infusion market was being eroded by increased competition as the health drink market broadened to include a much more mainstream consumer group looking for tasty products with a healthy, flavoursome image.

Springett Associates were appointed by Twinings to redesign new outer packaging and individual sachets which would appeal directly to this broader market and give the company's products greater shelf appeal in supermarkets.

The designers' solution was to use the packaging to communicate clear messages about the nature of the product and the rich range of its flavours. To do this, the simple cream of the original packages was changed for richly coloured diffused illustrations of the herbs, using the whole surface of each pack to evoke the flavour inside. The diffused style of the images echoes the nature of the infusions themselves and coveys a sense of the mystery and romance associated with the natural herbal recipes.

The colours and unique style of illustration have created high visibility for the products. Supermarket shelf presence has been significantly strengthened.

● *A new image for Twinings'*
Herbal Infusions
Designer: *Christine Simmons*
Art Director: *Peter Green*
Illustrator: *Christine Simmons*

● *A fresh new image for*
Premier Brands' Typhoo
Designers: *Rod Petrie*
and Steve Elliott
Art Director: *Rod Petrie*
Illustrators: *Bysouth and Hayter*

● **Design Bridge UK Limited**

When Premier Brands introduced foil packaging for their Typhoo tea it was felt it was time the brand's old surface design had a significant change of direction which would reflect this innovative new development.

Design Bridge, with their extensive knowledge of the brand and its history, were commissioned to work on this project.

Their first move was to dispense with the image of a traditional tea service, and replace it with an illustration of a simple tea leaf to communicate the freshness of the product. The typography on the brand name was also freshened up and made to look more contemporary.

● *Stylish design for Lyons Tetley's
established brand*
Designer: *Louise Wardle*
Art Director: *Joe Jones*
Illustrators: *Tony McSweeney,
Bob Venables, Ivan Allen and
Robin Heighway-Bury*

● **Jones Knowles Ritchie**

Lyons Tea is an established, familiar brand in Britain's High Streets, generally seen over the years as reliable and wholesome but a bit old-fashioned.

This new packaging counteracts these negative associations and positions the brand as a premium yet authentic product accessible to the mass market.

Particular attention was paid the typography in the design, in order to convey a more stylish personality. The individual illustrations relate to each tea's origins and their specific flavours.

The complete range is offered in department store restaurants, airports, cafes and other similar outlets. The range of packs forms an eye catching display designed to encourage consumers to experiment with different teas.

○ *Strong new designs for*
Lyons Tetley
Designer: *Simon Davidson*
Art Director: *Gerard O'Dwyer*
Photographer: *Laurie Evans*

○ The London Design Partnership

The introduction of de-caffeinated tea bags was a new venture for Lyons Tetley, one of the oldest tea producers in the UK.

The brief for the pack designs demanded that they communicate an authoritative personality to both the retail trade and the consumer, so that de-caffeinated tea would quickly be seen as an acceptable alternative to the British "cuppa".

The pack aims to appeal to mainstream tea drinkers who enjoy a full-flavour "real" tea, rather than to those looking for a health infusion.

Ian Logan Design

In this case, the designers were asked by Waitrose to create a pack design which would have an "Italian Espresso" feel and reflect the company's image as a quality retailer. The design would also have to compete with others in the range of coffees.

The solution was to use silver foil on the label and a silver lid for the jar. The Italian flag was used to convey the style and taste of the coffee.

● *Espresso Instant Coffee*
for Waitrose
Designer: *Stuart Colville*
Art Director: *Alan Colville*
Illustrator: *Nick Baxter*

● *Designs for a new kind of coffee for*
Edinburgh Coffee Company
Designer: *Ken Craig*
Art Director: *Ken Craig*
Photographer: *Ian Atkinson*
Illustrator: *Dovrat Ben-Nahum*

● Graphic Partners

The brief here was to develop packaging designs for the launch of a new organically grown coffee which would be available in both caffeinated and de-caffeinated varieties.

The product - the first of its kind to be sold in the UK - has been produced to capture a share of the 25/40-year-old environmentally and health conscious market; one which is always on the lookout for new and satisfying products.

The design solution uses a state-of-the-art valve pack combined with laminated foil to project the contemporary feel of the product. The overall colours of the surface design - white, hot reds, oranges, yellows and pinks - were deliberately chosen to evoke an image of the coffees' dramatic mountain origins.

● *A simple solution for*
Waitrose French Coffee
Designer: *Stuart Colville*
Art Director: *Alan Colville*
Illustrators: *Line & Line*

● **Ian Logan Design**

As part of their plans for their expanding range of coffees, Waitrose asked Ian Logan Design to create packs for their French varieties.

The designers produced this simple, sophisticated solution using stripes of colour which correspond to the French flag. The panels, with their obvious visual information, also represent the French flag colours when they are placed next to each other.

● *Collages for Safeway's*
  coffee designs
  Designer: *Lucy Drew*
  Art Director: *Mary Lewis*
  Photographer: *Carl Warner*

● **Lewis Moberly**

Though they are all ground from the finest Arabica beans grown on mountain slopes, the three rich, aromatic coffees in the Safeway range come from three different countries.

The design of the packs aims to project the atmosphere of each of the various regions through the use of photographic collages. The packs stand apart from the generally dark, sober colours associated with this retail sector, but retain the rich, seductive qualities of premium coffee packaging.

Snacks and Soft Drinks

T he market for snacks and soft drinks is immense in Britain, ranging from popcorn to potato crisps and fizzy drinks to fruit juices. This selection shows the level of invention needed to give consumer appeal to any brand and keep it riding high in its particular sales league.

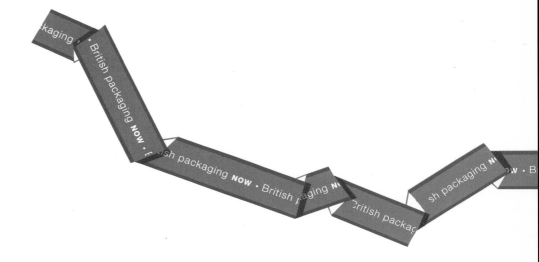

● *Pop packaging for Bards' popcorn*
Designer: *Belinda Duggan*
Art Director: *John Blackburn*
Illustrator: *Belinda Duggan*

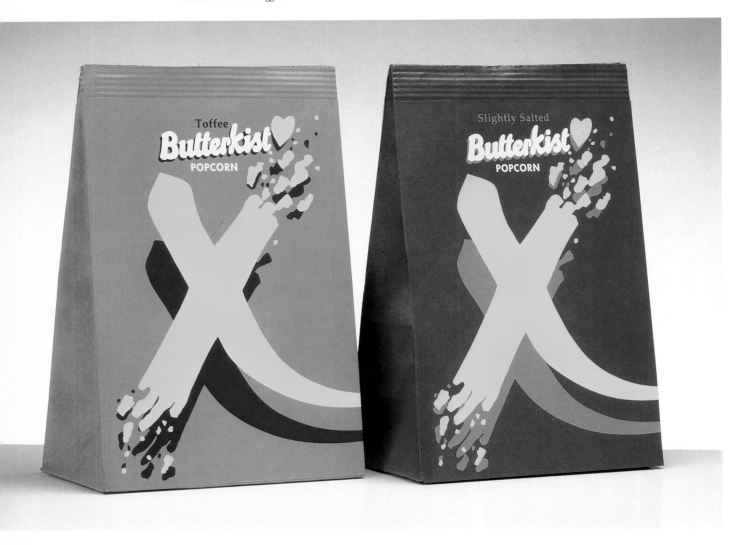

● Blackburn's Limited

Popcorn has long been sold as a fun, lively snack - almost as a commodity - rather than as a brand. As market leaders, Butterkist were uniquely placed to firmly establish themselves and their product as the undisputed number one in the market, by fending off the many other manufacturers and own-label competitors with a big, brave brand image they could clearly call their own.

The dynamic "popping kiss" embellished with a loving heart emphasises the fun in the product, reinforces the brand and gives it an instantly recognisable personality amongst its many competitors, whether they be savoury or sweet products.

• *Supermarket success for*
Franks Ice Cream Limited
Designer: *Rebecca Cochrane*
Art Director: *Nigel Daniels*
Illustrator: *Rebecca Cochrane*

● **Nick Holland Design Group**

Franks, a small family firm in Wales, have been making good quality ice cream for some years, but had been unsuccessful in their attempts to sell to large supermarket groups.

Nick Holland Design were commissioned to develop a classic new style of packaging for Franks which was key to the successful introduction of their products into the major quality supermarket chains in Britain.

● *Sammontana's new*
Gran Gelato range
Designers: *Ian Delaney*
and Jon Loader
Art Director: *Marcello Minale*

● **Minale, Tattersfield & Partners**

Sammontana, the Italian ice-cream giant, approached Minale Tattersfield with a brief to design the packaging for its new "Gran Gelato" range.

There are two sizes of pack - 2 litres and 1 litre - and a variety of mouthwatering flavours.

The new design, which is aimed at all ages, evokes the feel of the 1950s and 60s, of summer and the sea-side and a time when ice-cream was considered to be a special treat.

Chen Tsoi Design

Tesco asked that the packs for their new range of American-style ice cream should be bright and exciting with strong shelf impact.

The designers' solution was to use an American-influenced pop-art style of illustration and strong, dynamic typography. The stars and stripes device has been adapted and used on the pack lids while the typography and illustration follow the same format throughout the range, the only differentiation being made in the bold use of colour for each variety.

A pop art image for
Tesco's ice cream
Designer: *Kara Sims*
Art Director: *Chen Tsoi*
Illustrator: *Terry Hand*

Nettle Design Limited

American-style food is becoming increasingly popular in Britain, and it's not all hamburgers, fried chicken and ribs.

Traditional American ice cream is creamier than its English counterpart and comes in some unusual and exotic flavours. As part of their programme of own brand development, Asda have launched a range of four flavours of American-style ice cream featuring Amaretti Fudge Brownie, Triple Chocolate Sundae, Peanut Butter Crunch and Vanilla Fudge Chunk.

The design created for all the flavours evokes an image of the traditional American ice cream parlour. The Norman Rockwell style of the illustration, the strong branding in Tiffany lettering and the decorative devices all combine to project the idea of an all-American product.

American-style design for Asda Stores' ice cream
Designer: *Glyn West*
Art Director: *Glyn West*
Illustrator: *Peter Ross*

● *Timeless brand values*
for Clarke Foods
Designers: *Glenn Tutssel*
and Nick Hanson
Art Director: *Glenn Tutssel*
Photographer: *Andy Seymour*
Typographer: *Peter Horridge*

● Michael Peters Limited

The brand identity for this range of ice creams has been deliberately designed to reflect the values of Clarke Foods' existing and future business.

The sweeping calligraphic treatment of the new symbol conveys the creamy, luxurious quality of the product.

The background photograph on each pack is a collage of ephemera from Henry Clarke's archives mixed with other found objects.

The flavour differentiation has been achieved through the use of various initial letter forms.

The rich, dark packaging helps to endorse the product's position as a premium brand in its marketplace, whilst retaining a strong range identity.

● *Ice cream from Rinascente*
  of Milan
Designer: *David Pike*
Art Director: *Mary Lewis*
Photographer: *Paul Kemp*
Illustrator: *Geoffrey Appletona*

● **Lewis Moberly**

Based in Milan, La Rinascente is the oldest department store in Italy, with SMA as its food retailing outlet.

The packaging for SMA Ice Cream aims to reflect the Italians' age-old love affair with this dessert, with the ice cream itself as hero, spotlit by the logo with each variety of flavour performing its own unique act and focusing on its ingredients.

As a wide range with many flavours, it aims to create interest and project an appetising appeal in an imaginative, engaging way.

ASDA

6 REAL ORANGE LOLLIES
MADE WITH CONCENTRATED ORANGE JUICE

*No artificial
colours or flavours
No preservatives*

- **Elmwood Design Limited**

Asda commissioned Elmwood Design to create the packaging for a range of adult lollies with a high fruit juice content.
  The design solution centres on the product's ingredients, with images of orange groves suggesting freshly picked, high quality fruit. The detailed illustration of the lolly itself communicates the sense of a refreshing taste.

- *New designs for Asda's lollies*
Designer: *Clare Marsh*
Illustrator: *Ken Binder*

*An Olympic ice-cream for
Barcelona and Eismann*
Designer: *Judi Green*
Art Director: *Brian Green*
Photographer: *Andy Seymour*

● **The Green House**

España, a vanilla ice-cream bar containing muesli, was launched in six European countries by Eismann, a home delivery service and food manufacturer, specifically for the Barcelona Olympics.

The fact that this product is purchased from the Eismann catalogue and then delivered direct to the consumer set up unusual parameters for the designers to work within. Although the catalogue features all the company's products,

the product packaging is seen for the first time once it's been bought and delivered. Because of this, it was not necessary for the packaging to feature images of product usage and the designers thus had great scope for creative freedom.

Their objective was to bring the Eismann brand - which is relatively unknown in the UK - to life with a bold, fun design. They also wanted the brand to have a strong visual appeal and to compete well against other brands stored in home freezers. And the pack had to

communicate healthy, active brand values as well as the international qualities of the manufacturer.

The design is based on a background of brightly coloured national flags with the Olympic rings overlaid in gold. The España logo features Columna, a classic script typeface, with each letter picked out in a different Olympic colour to increase the overall impact.

The design solution creates a clear identity which can be used in several countries.

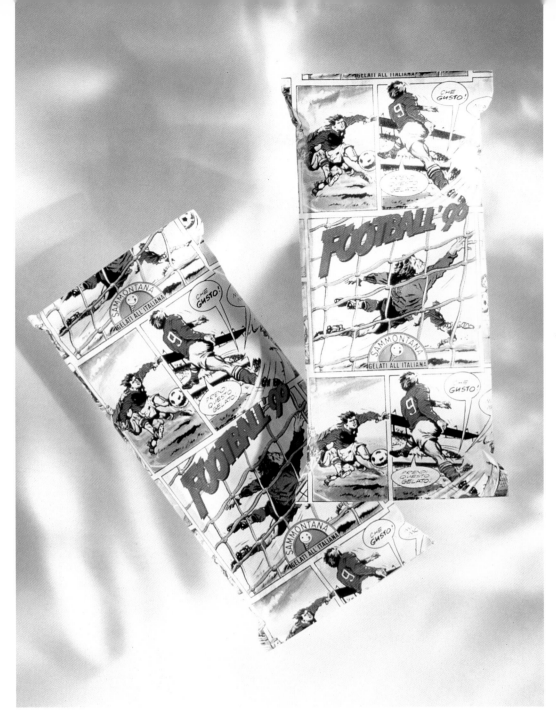

I n the true Italian style of
making even the most modest
products attractive, Sammontana
always encourage Minale
Tattersfield to give their packaging
an overall theme of elegance
wedded to a sense of fun.

The most recent of the more than
150 packs designed by Minale
Tattersfield have been highly
successful both visually and
commercially, with Sammontana
increasing their share of the
market by more than 100%.

The packs shown here belong to
the new Coppa D'Oro range and
the selection of lollies made for
children.

The continual up-dating of the
packs makes for maximum consumer interest in a highly competitive market; the lively and colourful illustrations make an immediate
impact and lasting impression on
adults and children alike.

● *Sammontana's ice creams
and lollies*
Designers: *Ian Delaney
and Marcello Minale Jnr*
Art Director: *Marcello Minale*

● The Green House

Eden Vale's Ski Bar is Britain's first hand-held frozen yoghurt bar.

The designs commissioned from The Green House had to present this product's unique properties both simply and with impact. Part of the challenge facing the designers was the need to create a personality which capitalised on the healthy, tasty image of the Ski yoghurt brand yet still positioned the Ski Bar as a new product able to fight for its own place in an crowded market.

Ski Bars are sold in newsagents and supermarkets, and have to compete with products like the Mars Ice Cream Bar. And Eden Vale wanted a design which also suit the European marketplace.

The solution was a hand-drawn script typeface for the word 'Bar' in blue with a silver dropped shadow, which complements the traditional dark blue of the Ski logo. The combination of this and the photographs of single fruits create an image of fresh quality.

Since its successful launch as a strawberry flavoured product, the Ski Bar range has been extended to include the peach and passion fruit and orange flavours featured here.

C adbury's Milk Drink was originally launched in packaging which failed to communicate the product's main advantage: its taste.

The Jenkins Group were briefed to produce new designs which would communicate this USP, and position the product as a refreshing milk drink containing real Cadbury's chocolate with the textural quality of a "liquid confection".

Cadbury wanted to retain their existing loyal customers, and attract impulse purchasers and infrequent users.

The designers researched the competition in the kinds of confectioners and newsagents where it is so often sold, and then designed a pack which would match the promise of the product within, using visual elements from the Cadbury's Milk Chocolate bar packaging.

The two chunks of appetising chocolate are eye-catching and convey the taste of real chocolate. The use of white on the pack helps to communicate the freshness of milk and the need to chill the product to appreciate it at its best.

● *An appetising new look for Premier Beverage Products*
Designer: *Ian Shillaker*
Art Director: *Ian Shillaker*
Photographer: *John Rawlings*

Blackburn's Limited

Cleeve's is the brand name for a new line of confectionery products re-launched by the Irish company, Clara Candy. It is a good example of packaging which is concept led rather than product led.

The Cleeve's products are generic to the confectionery business, and were already available as other major brands from companies like Rowntree and Trebor Bassett.

The packaging had to develop a lively, distinctive and individualistic image for the Cleeve's brand, if it was to have any impact in the market.

In the plethora of colourful packs - many of which are different but look the same - success for Cleeve's depended on the designers creating an image which would not disappear without trace.

The theme of the packaging is "thinking sweet thoughts", an idea which sprang from having to retain some elements of the existing Cleeve's logo - an oval with Cleeve's written in script, very much like the one used by Boots who also sell sweets. From the oval came the thought bubble, and from that the concept of "thinking sweet thoughts".

The cartoons by Gray Jolliffe are all different, but express the same idea: if you're feeling dull and grey, think of Cleeve's.

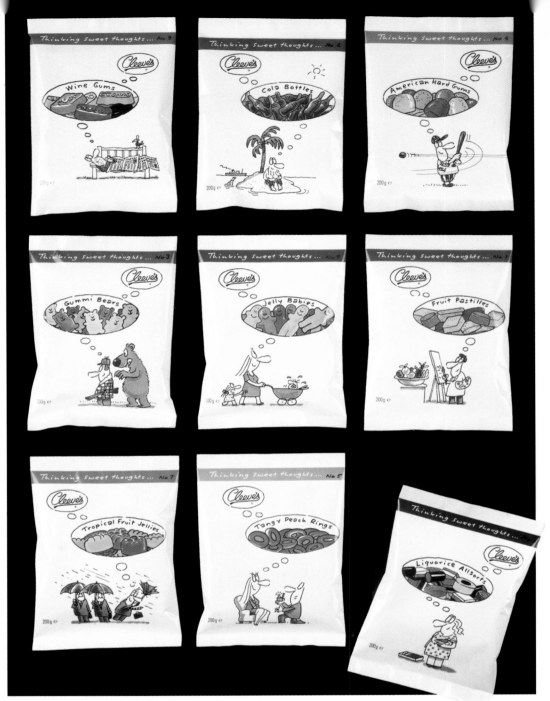

● *Conceptual packaging for*
Clara Candy Limited
Designer: *Belinda Duggan*
Art Director: *John Blackburn*
Illustrator: *Gray Jolliffe*

● *Mr Tom for Hosta Foods*
Designer: *Nin Glaister*
Art Director: *Mark Wickens*
Illustrator: *Melissa Grimes*

● **Wickens Tutt Southgate**

The launch in the UK of Mr Tom, a well-established German confectionery brand, called for a fresh identity which would appeal to youngsters in the 15/19-year-old age bracket.

Developing the brand as "the nutty bar with the nutty name", the designers introduced the "seriously nutty" line which carries through the packaging and into the advertising.

The obvious solutions of either showing the ingredients or inventing a Mr Tom character were rejected in favour of a design based on a collage of crazy images: monkeys on bicycles, strongmen with hippopotamus heads, acrobats, contortionists and the like.

The other "rules" of the confectionary market - a big, simple logo and strong colour combinations - were also rejected in favour of a design which stands out because it is so busy. And it looks busy whichever way you

look at it, and from whichever angle.

The "seriously nutty" theme has been carried through on all the packs, including the fun-size bars which are half the size of the 30g bar and have simply been cut in half - branding and all.

● *Vivid colours for*
Trebor Bassett's wine gums
Designer: *Belinda Duggan*
Art Director: *John Blackburn*
Illustrators: *Gilchrist Studios*

● Blackburn's Limited

For years wine gums were a much loved but forgotten sweet category.

Blackburn's decided to re-awaken an awareness of and interest in wine gums - and reinforce the Trebor Bassett brand - by creating a vivid and brightly coloured twist-wrap pack.

The rainbow design picks up the five colours of the different flavours; the soft, vignetted merging of the coloured stripes evokes the mouth-watering nature of the gums, while the overall identity projects just the right image of slightly sophisticated fun.

● *An evocation of the past for*
Cravens of York
Designer/Art Director: *Glyn West*
Photographer: *Alan Marsh*
Illustrator: *Roger Gorringe*

● **Nettle Design Limited**

The brief given to Nettle Design by Cravens of York was for a design for their sweets which would have impact at the point of sale in a crowded market, stimulate impulse purchases and reinforce the company's reputation as producers of high quality, traditional confectionery.

The design centres on a display panel which features an illustration of the sweets and the line "Remembering how things used to be". This links with a background photograph which, through its nostalgic selection of ephemera, is designed to evoke the target market's childhood

The re-design has generated excellent sales figures, and the concept has been adapted to suit other packaging forms.

● *A striking identity for Gruppo*
Rinascente's chocolate range
Designer: *Roger Akroyd*
Art Director: *Glenn Tutssel*
Photographer: *Alan Newnham*

● **Michael Peters Limited**

Gruppo Rinascente is one of
Italy's major retailers, marketing a range of own label products
which have a distinctive air of quality.
The design for this chocolate range
features a calligraphic initial drawn
from the product's name and a
photographic image which combine
to create a striking brand identity.

● **Michael Thierens Design**

Following the success of Michael Thierens' original designs for their chocolate bars, Waitrose decided to introduce a new range of continental bars. Manufactured in France to an old established recipe, these bars have a high cocoa content which yields a rich continental taste. They are aimed at the more luxurious end of the market.

The designers embellished a traditional European script and employed deckle edging to give the products a hand wrapped quality and evoke feelings of extravagance. The embossed seal adds to the sense of indulgence which prompts what is essentially an impulsive purchase.

Springett Associates

Terry's consumer research had revealed a gap in the boxed chocolate market for a product with appeal for young adults.

Recognising that 15-24 year olds were not attracted by the hearts and flowers imagery traditionally associated with boxed chocolates, Terry's asked Springett Associates to develop a brand which would directly target this age-group and visually shake up what had become a rather predictable product category.

The designers' approach was to move away from the conventional vocabulary of chocolate box design in favour of a complete revolution in shape, colour and performance. The brand identity had to come from the excitement of using the product. The structural packaging was the key.

Le Box has a carton designed to swivel, allowing the consumer to choose from both layers of exotic new chocolates at once. The graphics, based on the structure of the box itself, are bold and dynamic and add an element of fun and energy not previously associated with the chocolate box market.

Though this is a radical solution, it still retains the special qualities associated with any successful box of chocolates: mystery, romance, discovery, choice and indulgence.

● *A revolutionary approach
for Terry's Le Box*
Designer: *Sue Bicknell*
Art Director: *Rod Springett*

● *Terry's Pyramint range*
Designer: *Allison Miguel*
Art Director: *Mark Wickens*
Illustrator: *Harry Willock*

● **Wickens Tutt Southgate**

Terry's of York wanted to broaden the appeal of their Pyramint range, and position it at the more premium, self-indulgent end of the confectionery market. They also wanted the designers to give the brand added value, over and above its unusual pyramid shape.

The idea of imaginative indulgence was developed by creating eye-catching metallic packaging in gold, green and blue colours, each one a reinforcement of the product's smooth, cool minty taste.

The exotic imagery used on the pack's surface creates an alluring and imaginative pattern interlaced with four pyramids.

New-look after dinner mints
for Terry's of York
Designer: *Sean Langford*
Art Director: *Gerard O'Dwyer*

● The London Design Partnership

In this example the designers worked closely with Terry's of York in re-launching their range of after dinner mints.

In this sector of the confectionery market, where sweets are bought mainly as gifts, the physical appearance of any packaging is particularly important. Not only does the pack have to be appealing on the shop or supermarket shelf, it also has to look good on a dinner table.

The essential features of this design have been used on all the elements of the pack: the acetate lid, the inner tray, the foil wrap and so on.

● *Up-dating the Spartan brand*
for Terry's of York
Designer: *Denise Pardey*
Art Director: *Gerard O'Dwyer*

● **The London Design Partnership**

Spartan is a dark chocolate brand which has been marketed by Terry's of York for many years.

Popular with predominantly older people, it had been suffering from declining sales.

The designers' recommendation to Terry's of York was to re-position the brand by more closely associating it with the company's much larger selling brand, All Gold.

This would give Spartan an opportunity to broaden its market through being seen as part of a family of brands.

The design solution combines the visual qualities of the original pack with a presentational style more in keeping with today's market and the consumer's demands.

● *New bags from Baker's Street*
  for Sisterson Foods Limited
Designers: *John Blackburn*
and John Fordham
Art Director: *John Blackburn*
Photographer: *David Gill*
Illustrator: *Michael Frith*

● Blackburn's Limited

Sisterson Foods, part of the Derwent Valley Food Group, recognised the gap in the consumer market for a "new" premium quality savoury snack.

The range they developed initially included three products: Bagel Chips, Meze Sticks and Sicilian Toasts. Each one is a speciality snack based on an expert baking technique, hence the choice of name for the range: Baker's Street.

Each product pack features a different shop front with an individual character and personality. The Bagel Chips feature a Jewish Bakers shop called Frenkel's. The Meze Sticks use Spiros, a Greek delicatessen. The Sicilian Toasts have Luigi's - an Italian shop - as their motif.

The design of the gussets for these packs is unique in that they each carry a photograph of the product, thus simulating a window onto the contents of the bag. The pack

structure is also flat-bottomed, which is reminiscent of an old-fashioned deli-bag. This allows the packs to be displayed as free standing items creating a row of ethnic shops, each offering its own distinctive product. The shops are individually numbered, so this imaginary street has the potential for being extended into a wide variety of products within an overall brand identity.

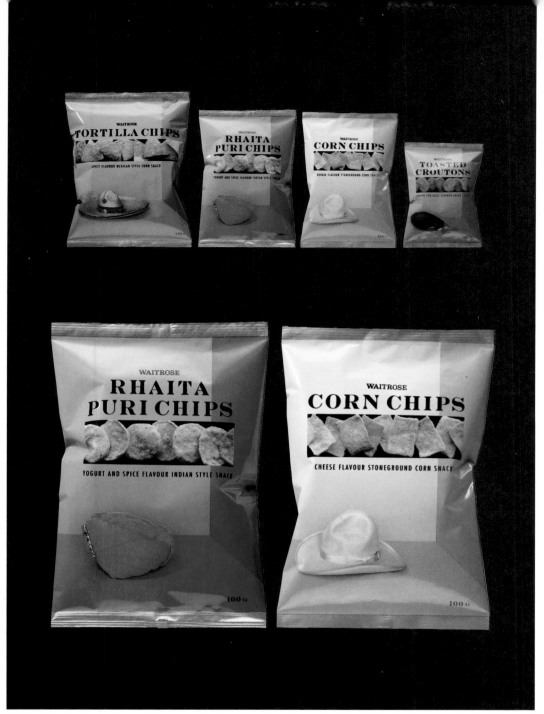

● Hats set the style for Waitrose's
round-the-world snacks
Designer: *Kathy Miller*
Art Director: *Kathy Miller*
Photographer: *David Stewart*

● Miller Sutherland

Waitrose's brief to Miller Sutherland called for four designs for premium snack products with a built-in "around the world" theme. The only competition they would face in-store would be from the established Phileas Fogg brand. So, while the packs had to compete in terms of quality, they could not be seen to be mimicking Phileas Fogg.

The packs also had to be clearly differentiated from each other, with each product visible on the front face of each pack. The final concept also had to allow for additional lines being introduced in the future.

By using hats as symbols of the country of origin, the range has a clearly international look. The stylish, slightly surreal photography places the hats in vibrantly coloured settings, thus clearly differentiating the products.

The simple but effective layouts promote the range's premium quality.

Trickett & Webb Limited

When Safeway briefed out the designs for their new range of speciality snacks there was only one restriction.

Despite wanting to associate the flavour of each product with its country of origin, maps were out for this range.

Recognising that snacks like these are most often eaten with a drink before dinner, the designers decided to explore the relationships between the snacks' various flavours and a variety of drinks labels associated with their countries of origin.

The result is an eye-catching series of packs for snacks such as garlic mini breads, which have a distinctly French flavour, chicken kiev nuggets, with their Russian connections, and spicy Mexican tortilla chips. The comparatively humble potato pipes draw their inspiration from British brown ale, while the pizza slices are cousins to a vermouth brand.

The packs, which are air filled to protect the contents, are printed in seven colours on matt finish foil which gives them the illusion of being made of glass.

With the exception of the product illustrations, all the artwork for the designs was generated in-house by Trickett & Webb soon after their computer systems had been installed.

• *Adult snacks for Safeway Stores, designed with drinks in mind*
Designers: *Andy Thomas, Lynn Trickett and Brian Webb*
Art Directors: *Lynn Trickett and Brian Webb*
Illustrators: *Andy Thomas and Robin Carter*

*One of four different images
for Smiths' Bloopers*
Designers: *Leo van Noppen
and Marcel Gort*
Art Director: *Eugene Bay*
Photographers: *Lex Verspeek
and Martin Woods*
Illustrator: *Leo van Noppen*

Visser Bay Anders Toscani

In this example, the simple brief from Smiths was to develop a new product which would be able to fight for attention in the already crowded youth snack market.

For the designers, the actual snacks were so nondescript and looked so much like a production mistake, it was decided to call them Bloopers - a concept which opened up endless possibilities for illustrating "faux-pas" situations.

A photographic and illustrative collage technique was developed, in the knowledge that young people would appreciate that kind of visual style. The idea of a series was made possible by creating four different Blooper moments and by printing them all at the same time from the same colour cylinder.

The product, which has been created for a three to four year life span in the youth market, has reinforced Smiths' image as a dynamic player in the savory snacks market.

● Michael Thierens Design

Since 1982 Derwent Valley Foods have established Phileas Fogg as the brand leader in the market for adult snacks. They were the first company to introduce tortilla chips to the UK. As part of their campaign to maintain their market lead, they asked Michael Thierens to re-design their entire range of snacks and subsequently to establish a series of new Phileas Fogg products.

Cool Tortilla is a less spicy and more aromatic product. This is reflected in the cool blue of the packaging, a colour not usually associated with food. The illustration was inspired by Punch cartoons of the 19th century. It emphasises the 'cool' theme whilst the 'joke' is continued in the established letter on the back of the pack from Phileas Fogg to his Aunt Agatha, enhancing the idiosyncratic nature of the product.

Pakora is the first of a new and more expensive range of products which have been developed to run along-side the original range. A more fluid design style was employed to allow for greater flexibility and variation in the future.

● *New Phileas Fogg products for*
Derwent Valley Foods
Designers: *Michael Thierens*
and Russell Hardingham
Art Director: *Michael Thierens*
Illustrator: *John Holder*

● *Making the most of Mexico*
and maize for Smiths
Designers: *Leo van Noppen*
and Eugene Bay
Art Director: *Eugene Bay*
Illustrator: *Leo van Noppen*

● **Visser Bay Anders Toscani**

The launch of Bugles introduced a new corn-based snack into the market; one aimed at the more discerning adult looking for something new to serve with lunchtime or early evening drinks.

Maize and Mexico combine well to create a product with a tasty promise, and the strong triangular maize symbol in the middle of the pack clearly differentiates Bugles from the mass of other potato snacks on the market. Nacho cheese rather than plain cheese adds to the product's exotic image.

Bugles now claims the number one position in the Dutch snacks market, with a massive 12% of sales. Its success in its home market has led to launches in a number of other European countries, and the establishment of Bugles as Smiths first pan-European brand.

● **Nettle Design Limited**

B udgens is a chain of small to medium sized supermarkets serving towns in the South East of England and the area around London. Their customers are mainly younger middle-class people who use the stores occasionally, because of their convenience, rather than for their weekly shopping.

Budgens' brief to Nettle Design called for strong colours to differentiate the products from one another. The design solution uses these colours in association with a graphic representation of the crisps.

The same design was also carried through to the individual 25 gramme packs which, although they would not be seen in the store, would act as a reminder of the Bugden brand once the six-pack was opened at home.

● *Strong colours on crisp packs*
for Budgens
Designer: *Sandy Palmer*
Art Director: *Glyn West*
Illustrator: *Sandy Palmer*

A powerful new identity for
the Smiths Food Group
Designers: *Leo van Noppen*
and Eugene Bay
Art Director: *Eugene Bay*
Photographer: *Martin Woods*

Visser Bay Anders Toscani

By the middle of the 1980s, the 100g packs of Smiths Chips in their two flavours were rapidly losing their share of the youth market.

Taking a radical view of the situation, the designers set about reversing the sales trend.

The almost industrially unfriendly image of the old packs was thrown out. The company name was relegated to make way for new branding and, instead of trying to

please everyone, the designers set out to please the kids.

Every aspect of the communications activity - pack design, advertising, point-of-sale - was drawn together to create a powerful new identity for the product.

Borrowing from satellite TV and video graphics - known visual grazing grounds for the chosen market group - the designers have used dynamic graphics on metal foil with appetising product photography on a white background.

Even the rule of always showing the product through the pack was broken. These chips are more crunchy than the competition, as their namestyle suggests.

Now the product comes in three flavours and in 175g packs, and is seen as a pioneer brand. Sales have exploded to a 40% market share, and Smiths are seen as leaders in their field.

● *Sophisticated soft drinks*
  for Waitrose
  Designer: *Kathy Miller*
  Art Director: *John Blackburn*
  Illustrator: *Geoff Appleton*

● Miller Sutherland/Blackburn's Limited

Waitrose wanted to create an adult-orientated range of soft drinks by marketing Fruit Crushes - drinks with a higher fruit content and more sophisticated flavours (such as Melon and Tropical) than the usual flavoured "pop". Although the products were to be a mainly adult purchase, they had to appeal to all ages groups and were expected to achieve their highest sales during the Summer months.

Blackburn's design solution avoids the cliches of most soft drinks imagery - bubbles and jazzy graphics - yet manages to convey the light-hearted and "fun" aspects of such drinks. In a series of colourful vignettes, the fruit becomes a beach ball at a 1940s holiday camp or beach scene. Typography reminiscent of Hollywood posters from the same era gives the packs an image which appeals to adults, while children can simply enjoy the utter daftness of playing ball with a melon.

This project was started by Kathy Miller while she was working for Blackburn's Limited and completed by her at Miller Sutherland.

● Saatchi & Saatchi Design

Saatchi & Saatchi first designed the Sunkist packs when the products were launched in the UK in 1989. Sunkist then went straight to number two in the orange drink market, and still retains this position.

The group was subsequently briefed to develop the design in order to build on the existing brand strengths, maintain good shelf stand out and, in particular, emphasise the natural orange values of the product.

This was achieved by adding "natural" imagery in the form of leaves and a green outer edging to the design, and subtly refining the shading and colours.

Research has shown that the new pack scores even more highly on shelf impact, "big brand" communication and overall appeal, with non-users showing a strong preference for the new design's natural orange emphasis.

The design has been followed through for the Diet version, where the branding and communication of the products natural qualities is equally strong and yet has a lighter feel.

● Tango for Britvic Soft Drinks
Designer: *Mark Wickens*
Art Director: *Mark Wickens*
Illustrator: *Steve Palmer*

● **Wickens Tutt Southgate**

Tango is the UK's answer to the welter of American soft drinks which flood the British market. Yet its original packaging did nothing to reflect this, or the product's sizeable share of the 16/24-year-old market.

The designers' research showed that the brand was more streetwise and modern than its previous design suggested.

The new design centres on the core proposition of a drink with a "tangy bite". The can shows an effervescent orange topped by a ring pull against a black background. The vibrant combination of colours not only gives the can powerful shelf impact, but also suggests a harder edge to the product and hints at its tangier flavour.

The strong, fizzing fruit and ring pull symbol allow the brand personality to work across all seven fruit flavours.

The Tango logo has also ben redesigned, again using an effervescent graphic style.

● *A sophisticated image for Panda Drinks' Rio Riva*
Designer: *Michael Thrasher*
Art Director: *Michael Thrasher*
Illustrator: *Peter Tunstall*

● Michael Stewart Design Limited

The Rio Riva range of soft drinks, made with pure spring water and fruit juice with no artificial sweeteners, colourings or preservatives, was launched by Panda Drinks in 1990 to meet the needs of the adult soft drinks market.

The brief to the designers called for work which would convey the purity of the ingredients and their cool, refreshing values whilst delivering all the impact of the "power brands" in a highly competitive marketplace.

The solution is a stylish graphic portrayal of Rio Riva's integrity, its clean, refreshing taste and adult sophistication in a much more direct way than was first developed by the major brands in the 1960s.

The colours are vivid and evoke the appeal of fresh fruit. The clean white background conveys purity and gives each can a strong visual impact at the point of sale.

Marketed in four flavours, the cans are printed in white with an additional five or six colours - the maximum available in the canning industry. Innovative production techniques were needed to achieve the colour values of real fruit, with all six colours being applied at a speed of 1,500 cans per minute without any cross contamination of the printing inks.

The entire pack emphasises the brand's integrity in the environmentally conscious 90s. The pure aluminum one-trip pack is 100% recyclable, with a litter-conscious stay-on tab. A donation is made to the World Wild Life Fund for every can sold.

Elmwood Design Limited

Wanting to distance themselves from the typically retrospective designs so often used in the traditional lemonade sector of the soft drinks market, Macaw preferred to concentrate on the quality of their ingredients and the fullness of their product's taste.

The basket brimming with lemons suggests a product bursting with flavour. And, with its contemporary colourways, the detailed illustration gives the labels a sense of quality and a feeling of today rather than the 1950s.

The flying Macaw logo adds an amusingly quirky touch to the label.

● *Macaw's traditional lemonade*
Designers: *Clare Marsh and Julia White*
Art Director: *Julia White*
Illustrator: *John Richardson*

● *A successful new image for*
Cadbury Schweppes' French Gini
Designer: *Jim Waters*
Art Director: *Jim Waters*

● Minale, Tattersfield & Partners

Gini was first launched on the French market in 1970, and had not had a change of packaging or identity since then. However, as an established brand with budding international ambitions, Gini had to be prepared to face stronger brand competition if it was to succeed in its new markets.

The designers' brief was to create a pack which would appear more dynamic and be able to join the mainstream mould whilst main-taining the personality of the original design.

With its brighter background colour, the new packaging suggests sparkle and freshness; the stylised leaf underlines the brand name and gives it a slightly exotic look.

Tests carried out on both sides of the Channel have shown that the new identity and packaging have not only succeeded in re-positioning Gini in the French market, but have also fulfilled the expectations of the British consumer.

● *A major up-date for*
Barr's IRN-BRU
Designers: *Ian Grindle*
and Bruce Duckworth
Art Director: *Ian Grindle*

● **Minale, Tattersfield & Partners**

IRN-BRU is one of Scotland's best-known soft drinks.

Minale Tattersfield's brief was to re-design the product's packaging in line with AG Barr's plans to introduce it into other regional markets of the UK and Europe.

The original designs had unique characteristics which had long been associated with the brand. These have been successfully maintained and blended into this new design to give the drink the look of a major brand.

Minale Tattersfield's work has been well supported by the style of advertising adopted for IRN-BRU over the last few years.

Turner Duckworth

The brief for the re-design of Rose's Original Lime Juice Cordial was the designers' perennial problem: how to reconcile traditional style with contemporary production methods.

The traditional Rose's pack had, for years, been a delicately embossed bottle which - in order to rationalise the company's production - was to become a simple, square plastic container.

Turner Duckworth made a number of alterations to the traditional Rose's roundel, including the addition of the description "Original", and positioned it at the centre of a full length label which had been designed to cover the container's unsightly ribbing. The remainder of the label was covered with intricate embellishments which include the story of Lauchlan Rose, the drink's inventor.

Post-launch research confirmed that the consumer's perception, understanding and appreciation of the brand's quality had actually increased.

● *A new look for a traditional cordial*
  for Coca-Cola Schweppes
  Designer: *David Turner*
  Art Director: *David Turner*
  Illustrator: *John Pilley*

Design with a Far Eastern theme
for Greenbank Drinks Company
Designer: Kathy Miller
Art Director: John Blackburn
Photographer: David Gill

● **Miller Sutherland/Blackburn's Limited**

Amé is the premier brand of the Greenbank Drinks Company. Pronounced "Ah-may" - Japanese for "gentle rain" - it is a new adult soft drink based on herbal extracts, fruit juices, vitamins and minerals. It is aimed at the sophisticated adult sector of the market and recognises their requirement for a drink that does more than simply quench one's thirst or refresh one's well-being.

The design solution evokes Eastern themes through the use of colours, textures and the simplicity of form associated with Japanese art. The ingredients and their benefits have been described in detail on the front of the bottle, thus emphasising the special nature of the product. The carefully controlled imagery and elegant shape of the pack have established Amé right at the top of a highly competitive market, and have enabled Greenbank to exceed all their initial sales targets and challenge worldwide brands such as Aqualibra.

This project was started by Kathy Miller while she was working at Blackburn's Limited and completed by her at Miller Sutherland.

Pemberton & Whitefoord

This individual, fresh and lively packaging for Tesco's whole orange drink introduces a good deal of style and wit into the chill cabinet display.

Mimicking the individual fruit's peel, the carton design has enough scope to be extended across a very wide range of whole fruit drinks.

The product information has been styled as if it were a fruit label, and the hole for the straw has been positioned where the stalk would have been.

A fresh and lively approach for Tesco's whole fruit drinks
Designer: *Liz Piper*
Art Directors: *Simon Pemberton and Adrian Whitefoord*

• *A clear image for San Pellegrino's
new Mirage juices*
Designers: *Ian Delaney
and Marcello Minale*
Art Director: *Marcello Minale*
Illustrator: *Rosanne Sanders*

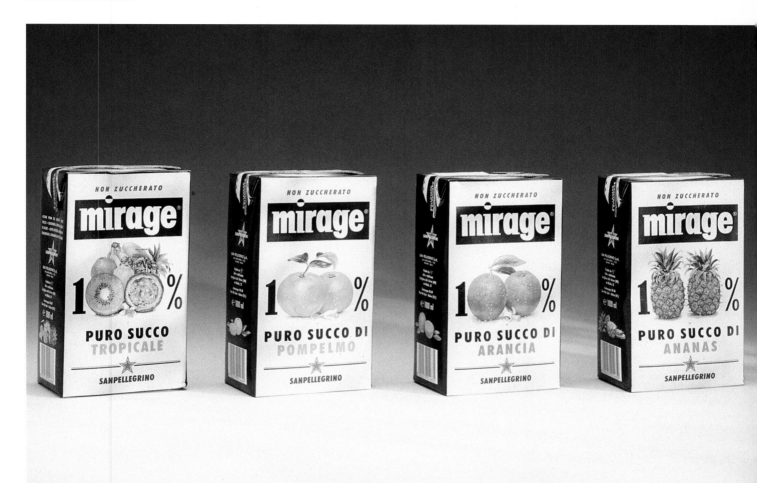

• Minale, Tattersfield & Partners

M inale Tattersfield's long-
standing client, San
Pellegrino, has recently introduced
a new range of 100% pure fruit
juices in a range of flavours.

Aimed at the new breed of health-
conscious and additive-averse
consumers, Mirage fruit juices
contain no additives whatsoever -
a fact simply and effectively
communicated by the design of
the packs.

There are four juices in the range -
orange, grapefruit, pineapple and
tropical - with the relevant fruits
clearly illustrated on the pack leaving
no doubt as to the contents.

NOW • British

British packaging NOW • British

ng NOW • British

NOW • British packaging NOW • B

kaging NOW • Brit

ckaging NO

kaging NC

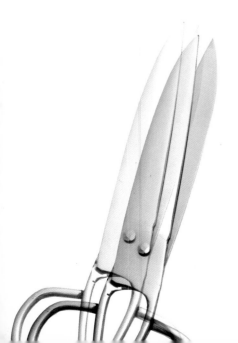

● Alcoholic Drinks and Tobacco

Many of Britain's brewers and distillers compete in crowded markets overseas as well as having to face stiff competition at home. For them, as for the supermarkets who sell so many own label wines and spirits, good packaging has to project the right image to the right people.

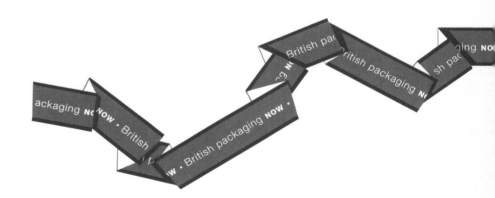

● *The "Cutty Sark" comes to life*
for Berry Brothers & Rudd
Designer: *Belinda Duggan*
Art Director: *John Blackburn*
Illustrator: *Jean Paul Tibbles*

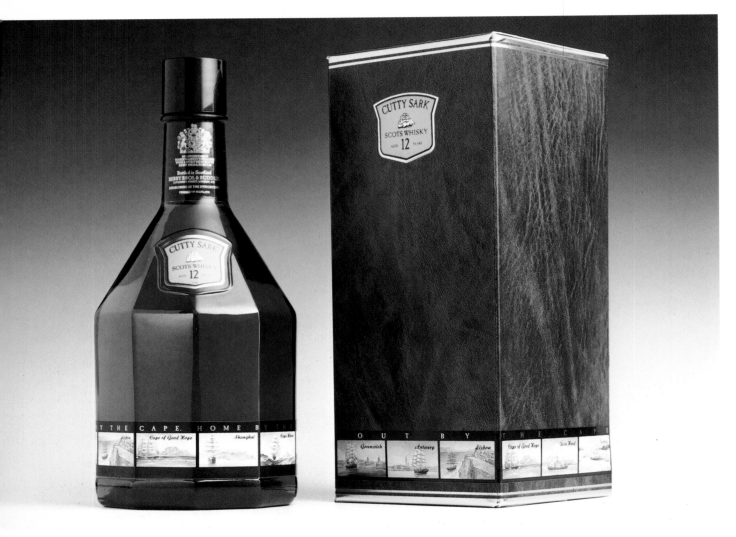

● **Blackburn's Limited**

The packaging for this twelve-year-old whisky exploits the achievements of the last of the great tea clippers, the famous "Cutty Sark", and her record-breaking circumnavigation of the world: "Out by the Cape, home by the Horn".

The unique ten-sided bottle allows this romantic story to unfold, with each of the facets depicting the ports of call from Greenwich to The Lizard by way of Antwerp, Lisbon, The Cape of Good Hope, Java Head, Sydney, Hong Kong, Shanghai, Cape Horn, Rio de Janeiro and New York - each one a destination which today markets Cutty Sark whisky.

Green was chosen to reflect the colour of the sea, acting as a natural backdrop for the specially created Cutty Sark shield, developed by Blackburn's from the distinctive large yellow label of the standard brand. This now features on all corporate expressions of the company's identity, and will do so on future brands as they develop.

● **Blackburn's Limited**

This ten-sided bottle, which is unique to Cutty Sark whisky, emphasises the rich colour of this rare eighteen-year-old malt, yet allows the etched illustration of the famous "Cutty Sark" clipper to come sailing through on the back of the bottle.

Both are supported by the Cutty Sark shield developed by Blackburn's from the large and distinctive yellow label of the standard brand.

The yellow ribbon picks up this theme and positions the brand as a luxury gift within the Cutty Sark portfolio, and against other brands in international markets - especially the Far East.

Each bottle carries a neck booklet and is enclosed in a black, ten-sided gift box. Both the booklet and the box feature "Sayings of the Sea" by romantic writers such as Byron, Coleridge, Horace, Swinburne and Longfellow.

Graphic Partners

The plan to extend the range of Invergordon Distillers' Cluny whiskies to include 17 and 21-year-old blends for the North American and Far Eastern markets - and in particular the specific requirements of the Japanese - called for a new approach to the brand's packaging.

The basis for the design solution is an old Cluny label from the early 1900s which, it was felt, expressed many of the values and qualities required for the new blends. In its contemporary treatment, many of its devices, such as heraldic emblems and decorative borders, have been re-drawn in keeping with a more modern image. This, and the use of embossing and metallic finishes, has resulted in an identity which cleverly combines features from the old world and the new.

Almost identical labels were used for the two whiskies, differentiated only by age and colour. A tall, straight, round bottle was also used for both blends, with a specially designed neck label around the foot of each capsule to heighten the value of the product.

In both cases, a high standard of finish was achieved through the use of gloss and matt varnishes, embossing and the ornate shape of the labels which are printed on foil stock.

● *A quality image for Invergordon's aged blends*
Designer/Art Director: *Ron Burnett*
Illustrator: *James Gorman*
Calligrapher: *David Lang*

Integrated design for
William Lundie's Lismore Scotch
Designer: *Graham Duffy*
Art Director: *Graham Duffy*

● **Graphic Partners**

William Lundie's brief to Graphic Partners was to reposition and re-launch the Lismore range of blended whiskies for distribution in the Duty Free markets of the Far East. The range includes twelve, fifteen and eighteen-year-old blends, and was extended to include a standard blend for the US market and an eight-year-old blend for Europe.

Graphic Partners' development of the new brand image was an integrated design project involving the creation of a new bottle and stopper and new labels, graphics, capsule and gift carton designs.

The squat shape of the bottle, with its full, deep shoulders and the wide base to its neck, falls between the standard tall, round bottle and the traditional dump bottle. The new shape suggests a full, rounded quality whisky while the "dead leaf" green

glass of the bottle gives a rich subtlety to the colour of the contents.

All the detailing in the label design combines to project an image of a product which has all the virtues of traditional strength and contemporary elegance. This is repeated on the twelve-year-old gift carton which has an olive and gold finish which matches the colour of the whisky in its bottle.

Darrell Ireland

I t was clear from the briefing that the creation of a new character for J&B Reserve, a 15-year-old blended Scotch whisky, would have to be carried out within a tight budget. The shape of the bottle and label were already set, the client's current tooling would have to be used and the label's visual appearance would have to link in with J&B Rare, one of the top-selling whiskies in the world.

One fortunate advantage for the designer was the way the colour of the rich, amber liquid fused with the antique colour of the glass. Choosing the background colour and type for the label was comparatively easy. Only the final crafting of the typographic detail proved difficult.

As for the outer carton, the idea for the wood finish came from an opportunity few designers would have had: the chance to travel from Leeds to London with the Managing Director of J&B. All manner of ideas were bounced around during the journey, until Darrell Ireland came away with a strong feeling about what should be done. The following day he scoured specialist veneer shops until he found a suitable sheet of walnut burr, which a model-maker then carefully sanded and polished before the result was photographed and the image retouched.

- A new character for
Justerini & Brooks' J&B Reserve
Designer: *Darrell Ireland*
Art Director: *Darrell Ireland*

● *Justerini & Brooks' 20-year-old*
whiskey for Japan
Designers: *Darrell Ireland*
and Melonie Ryan
Art Director: *Darrell Ireland*

● **Darrell Ireland**

The brief for this project was simple yet - at the outset - seemingly impossible.

Darrell Ireland had just one month to produce initial concepts and approved finished artwork for all the packaging for a limited edition of a 20-year-old blended Scotch whisky to be sold solely in Japan.

The container is a ceramic flagon made by Royal Doulton. The decoration is a design chosen "off-the-shelf" for the way it conveys an appropriate image. The traditional neck hanger was designed with modest decorations, and the outer pack was created to reflect the bottle's personality.

The result is eye-catching and distinctive, and has established a new brand category for J&B.

● McIlroy Coates Limited

W hen Bass commissioned McIlroy Coates to design the packaging for a new brand of whisky, their brief was very clear.

Deerstalker had to exude heritage and tradition yet avoid the obvious whisky clichés.

The use of a 1926 Atholl Stalker photograph, rather than the ubiquitous stag, immediately creates a distinctive personality for the brand; one which is further reinforced by simple typography and the understated use of colour.

● *Traditional themes for*
Bass Export's new brand of whisky
Designers: *Graham Scott*
and Evan Hawkins
Art Directors: *Graham Scott*
and Ian McIlroy
Photographer: *Unknown*

● *Design with a Speyside origin*
for Tesco Stores
Designer: *Lindsay Herbert*
Art Director: *Glyn West*
Illustrator: *Lindsay Herbert*

● **Nettle Design Limited**

The aged whisky market has been growing over the past few years, with new brands and own label products being introduced all the time.

The Tesco whisky shown here is produced at a Speyside distillery in Scotland, and has a label design which - on both the 70cl and 35cl bottles - features an image which evokes that part of the country.

Hand lettering for the brand name and a decorative 10-year-old designation complete a design which reflects the quality of this product.

Peter Windett & Associates

The brief for this project was to create a new design for the Glenmorangie Ten Year Old Cask Strength whisky bottle and tube, keeping it clearly identifiable as part of the Glenmorangie tradition whilst portraying the distinctive qualities of this full strength whisky.

With its black and tan cartographer's edge, the central vignette of the distillery is taken from an archive photograph. The choice of colours - the parchment ground, the tan, red and green - is warm, natural and traditional, as is the ribbon, with the decorative words "Single Highland Malt Whisky", which supports the distillery image.

- A new design for Glenmorangie
  Ten Year Old Whisky
  Designer: Peter Windett
  Art Director: Peter Windett

Hiram Walker's brief to the designers was for a package and brand identity for a Bourbon whisky to be launched in the UK. The brand already existed in the USA, but its packaging was felt to be inappropriate for the British market.

The visual references and typefaces chosen all come from the traditions of early American advertising. Printed on a parchment ground (with the same effect created on the tin), the eagle marks the product as proudly American, especially with the banner it holds bearing the words "America's Native Spirit". The colours of red, tan, black and gold are bold and vital and, together with the reproductions of the old Hiram Walker distillery on the back label, combine to invest the product with an authentic, original feel.

● *Ten High Bourbon whisky
for Hiram Walker*
Designers: *Wendy Gardiner
and Peter Windett*
Art Director: *Peter Windett*

*A family feel for Invergordon's
Stillman's Dram*
Designer: *Ron Burnett*
Art Director: *Ron Burnett*
Illustrator: *Alyson MacNeill*
Calligrapher: *Donald Shannon*

Graphic Partners

The Stillman's Dram range of whiskies includes mature versions of five of Invergordon's whiskies - four single malts and one single grain - each with a distinctive brand identity.

Graphic Partners' brief was to develop new and coherent packaging for all the whiskies in the range. The objective was to retain some of the existing brand identities whilst at the same time giving them a new family feel. The solution was to give each bottle a primary and secondary label.

The first, placed just below the shoulders of the bottle, contains the overall Stillman's branding which employs elegant, distinctive script lettering and an illustration of the still. The label is printed on laid paper with a deckled edge and each label is individually numbered.

The second carries the existing brand identity, with the whisky's age clearly marked, to ensure instant recognition.

The overall brand identity is achieved by the use of mock wax seals, ribbons in varying colours and a swing neck tie, according to the blend.

Blackburn's Limited

To celebrate their £15m investment programme at their Portland factory in Scotland, Rockware Glass commissioned Blackburn's to design a unique commemorative bottle to be presented to leading representatives of the spirits industry. The bottle - which was to contain a rare, high quality thirty-year-old malt whisky - had to express the company's innovative skills, its excellent standards of production and its decorative expertise.

The highly distinctive result combines the traditional whisky values with both creative and technical innovations.

The recipients were asked to guess the origin of the 30-year-old malt, from a series of clues on the bottle and in the presentation box.

The name given to this rare gift was "Diomhair'Eachd", which is Gaelic for "mystery".

The clues are: *The Mysterious source which lies within; A mere stone's throw where ancient foes, no mercy spent; Once repulsed from fortress rock; As homing pigeons fly due north less six its very age; The message discerned by either stiff or nip reveals its very home.*

A small, decorative neck label displays the whisky's age.

● *Packaging a mystery for*
Rockware Glass
Designers: *John Blackburn*
and Belinda Duggan
Art Director: *John Blackburn*

Lewis Moberly

The launch of the Oban brand was a deliberate move to capitalise on one of the fastest growing sectors in the spirits market: malt whisky.

The sector offers consumers a broad choice in terms of flavour, appearance, price, origin, age and strength. Research into consumer attitudes reveals an adventurous customer type, interested predominantly in quality and willing to buy a brand which may rely for it success on an acquired taste.

The packaging brief called for an emphasis on the individuality of the fourteen-year-old malt which was to be projected through the bottle shape, the label, cork, cap and carton. The new brand had to be invested with authenticity, heritage, quality and a particular distinction.

The designers spent some time at the Argyll distillery, researching the history of the area in order to build a story around the product.

Oban overlooks the Firth of Larne, with the island of Mull in the distance. The graphics reflect the bleak rocky coast with its squawking gulls and bracing winds, while the label tells the story of the region and its distillery, aiming to bring a "bookish" feel to the brand.

● *A new brand steeped in history for United Distillers*
Designer: *Mary Lewis*
Art Director: *Mary Lewis*
Illustrator: *Bill Sanderson*

● **Lewis Moberly**

S ograpeare owners of the
famous Mateus brand, one
of the world's most popular wines,
currently selling at the rate of over
3 million cases a year.

Reserva is Sogrape's highest
quality wine.

The use of calligraphic type
creates a hand crafted image which
reflects the wine's quality through
its label. The different coloured
inks which flow into one another
draw attention to key elements in
the copy in a subtle way.

● *An image of quality for*
Vinhos Sogrape Reserva
Designer: *Mary Lewis*
Art Director: *Mary Lewis*

Blackburn's Limited

S wanson is a new Californian wine company. Its owner, Clarke Swanson Jnr., recently purchased a vineyard in the Napa Valley, adjacent to the renowned Robert Mondavi Winery, the producer of the famous Opus 1. This makes the Swanson Vineyard one of the most exclusive wine growing sites in the world.

Swanson commissioned Blackburn's to produce both a corporate identity and packaging designs for his range of wines.

The monogram seen on the neck of each bottle is the corporate logo: a double "S", one larger and one smaller, which effectively conveys the concept of Swanson & Son.

The label design depicts a profile of the son with the swan motif creating the boy's hair.

The range of wines is clearly positioned as being from the New World; at a glance, their stark, graphic simplicity separates them from the European competitors.

• *A New World design for Swanson Vineyards*
Designer: *John Blackburn*
Art Director: *John Blackburn*
Illustrator: *John Fordham*

*Distinctive design for
Gilbey de Loudenne*
Designers: *Darrell Ireland
and Robert Barton*
Art Director: *Darrell Ireland*

● **Darrell Ireland**

The concept behind the creation of La Môde Americaine was simple: quality-produced wine prepared under the guidance of an American viniculturist using only the most modern wine technology (which has never been used outside the USA's wine producing states before).

Gilbey de Loudenne decided that, to get this message across to the discerning customer, a straight-forward explanation of each wine

and its unique peculiarities should feature as a strong element in the packaging for the range. It was also decided that a strong brand logo should be created, and that elements such as the date of bottling and the wine varietals should be combined to project this unique mix of French and American attitudes towards wine making.

After some initial research, an existing Gilbey's bottle mould was selected from the company's bottle resource centre. Embellished with

the family crest, it helped to provide a final choice for the label decorations: a series of early 19th century engravings.

The mix of styles and individual characters has helped to establish each varietal as a distinctive member of a cohesive family of unique wines.

● *Strong colours for*
the Co-op's Spanish wines
Designer: *Elaine Morgan*
Art Director: *Elaine Morgan*
Illustrators: *Elaine Morgan*
and Jane Dodds

● Co-operative Wholesale Society Limited

The range of eight own label Spanish wines introduced by the Co-op includes four up-market wines - a red and white Rioja and a red and white Navarra - and four table wines.

As with any wine label design, the principal restraints revolve around the relationships between the elements of the copy. For example, "Navarra" is the dominant factor for two of the wines, so its size governs the size of "Vina Anaita", the D.O. statement and everything else.

Similarly, the designs must allow for the regional stamp or crest, which is overprinted by the supplier at source.

On the Rioja label, the abstract "flamenco" theme of swirling skirts and Spanish guitars uses actual Spanish artifacts glued onto a parchment base and then photographed to give it a three-dimensional effect.

The image of the bull on the Navarras was used to reinforce the full-bodied character of the wines. The original illustrations for the rough designs used a mixture of airbrush, crayon and montage. The client did not want these to be diluted in the translation into print, so they were re-drawn in exactly the same way again.

The consistency of the layout for both Rioja and Navarra labels was carried through to the table wines to give a family feel to the entire range.

Carroll Dempsey & Thirkell

Marks & Spencer wanted a design for its Californian wines which would cut through the mystique of wine buying and appeal to a younger, more adventurous market.

The designers drew their inspiration from the faded colours and artless lettering of the Hawaiian shirts of the 1950s. Their relaxed, informal mood chimes perfectly with the image of Californian sun, sand and surf, and the frame of mind in which the wines are best enjoyed. On the other hand, the classic typography suggests the inherent quality of the wine and brings together an overall approach which is at once both radical and traditional.

● *Marks & Spencer's Californian wines*
Designer: *Neil Walker*
Art Director: *Nicholas Thirkell*
Photographer: *David Timmis*
Illustrator: *Mick Brownfield*
Embroiderer: *Shelly Faye Lazar*

● *Sandeman's bi-centenary port*
Designer: *Paul Davies*
Art Director: *David Wombwell*

● Ziggurat Design Consultants

This strictly limited edition of Sandeman's 30-year-old Tawny Port was produced to celebrate the bi-centenary of the Sandeman family's successful business.

To commemorate this unique occasion, Ziggurat created a hand-blown replica of the very first bottle used by Sandeman, and decorated it with individually numbered, hand-crafted labels printed on fine laid paper and blind and foil embossed.

The letterpress printing gives the labels the quality and feel of antique book pages which is enhanced by the typographic style with its indented margins and use of both italics and upper-case letters.

The overall impression created by the packaging has no suggestion of artificial nostalgia, but presents the product's heritage in an entirely contemporary way.

Tesco's own-label cognacs needed identities which would suggest quality and authenticity at a reasonable price.

The solution to the problem lay in the use of classic typography and strong colours to differentiate between the two alternative cognacs.

● *Conveying quality and cost for Tesco's cognac*
Designer: *Tony Enoch*
Art Director: *Gerard O'Dwyer*

● **Michael Peters Limited**

The brief here was to develop an international brand identity for Martell which could be consistently used worldwide on packaging for the company's entire range of products.

The house martin symbol was developed into a worldwide logo to be used as a corporate identifier and as a brand identity on packaging.

New bottle shapes and, in some cases, new gift boxes were designed to add value to the products and thus justify their premium pricing.

● *A universal identity for Martell*
Designer: *Mark Pearce*
Art Director: *Glenn Tutssel*

Design Bridge UK Limited

The brief given to Design Bridge for the Hennessy Cuvée project centred on the need to communicate the difference in rank between VSOP and Cuvée Superieure "as unmistakably as possible".

Hennessy Cuvée Superieure is a grade above VSOP, and is designed to be sold exclusively in the expensive hostess bars and clubs frequented by businessmen in Japan. The brand's premium qualities are reflected in its price, which is twice that of VSOP.

The re-design involved the creation of a new bottle, and new graphics for the label and presentation box.

Design Bridge opted for a streamlined, elegant bottle shape to communicate the sophistication of the brand.

The label is still the traditional Hennessy oval. A "cut" down the middle of the bottle supports and gives prominence to the brand. The carton is rich "Cuvée Red", a colour which exudes luxury and wealth.

The overall presentation is in tune with today's ideas, not old-fashioned or staid, and offers credible Hennessy values.

● *A sophisticated design for*
Hennessy Cuvée Superieure
Designers: *Rod Petrie*
and Steve Elliott
Art Director: *Rod Petrie*
Typographer: *Steve Elliott*

*A unified range of liqueurs
for Giovanni Buton*
Designers: *Sherine Raouf
and Carrie Cummins*
Art Director: *Glenn Tutssel*
Illustrator: *Harry Willcok*

● **Michael Peters Limited**

Giovanni Buton's brief to Michael Peters was for pack designs to launch a range of six Italian liqueurs into the worldwide market, investing each one with an authentic, traditional yet idiosyncratic quality whilst still retaining a common, unifying identity for them all.

The solution centres on the use of a single bottle structure and a neck label which features the Buton signature. Together, the bottle and label hold the range together and communicate a singular house style.

● **Michael Peters Limited**

The chiselled typography, hand-crafted calligraphy and photographic detail of the satyr from Michelangelo's Bacchus bring an elegant look to the packaging for this Metodo Champenois from Italian drinks manufacturer, Giovanni Buton.

This particular combination of elements was chosen for the way in which they reflect the product's Italian origins.

● *Italian elegance for Giovanni Buton's metodo champenois*
Designer: *Glenn Tutssel*
Art Director: *Glenn Tutssel*
Photographer: *Sandy Porter*
Calligrapher: *Peter Horridge*

Michael Peters Limited

This American brand of vodka for a chain of bars and restaurants required a distinctive, relevant brand identity.

The target market for Tsaritsa was known to be vodka aficionados who prefer their drink straight from the ice box, hence the designer's choice of a bottle with a special frosting effect and a unique "wipe over" device through which consumers can see the label at the back of the bottle.

Tsaritsa Vodka for
D'Amico & Partners
Designer: *Glenn Tutssel*
Art Director: *Glenn Tutssel*
Illustrator: *Harry Willock*

KULOV

V O D K A

QUALITY SPIRIT
PRODUCED & BOTTLED IN THE UK
KULOV DISTILLERS, AIRDRIE

37.5% vol   70cl

● Ashted Dastor Associates

K ulov Distilleries is a small,
independent concern with
only a local presence in the
vodka market.

Their brief to Ashted Dastor was
for a design concept which would
establish an identity for their
product and allow it to compete
against the better-known brands
by giving it a much higher profile
in the market.

This individualistic design
uses imaginative graphics in an
interesting blend of Russian
constructivism and bold, eye-
catching typography.

The overall effect has enhanced
the drink's image and increased its
appeal amongst younger, visually-
orientated and style-conscious
consumers.

● A constructive solution
for Kulov's vodka
Designer: *Ashted Dastor*
Art Director: *Ashted Dastor*

The Team

The designs for this range of four premium sherries, regarded by the producers as "rare jewels, only available in small quantities", had to reflect the unique nature of the product.

The designers were asked to portray an image of nobility and quality, clearly distinguishing the sherry variants through colour coding of the hand marbled backgrounds and capsules.

The identification of the dry to medium dry qualities of the product also had to be made clear.

The result is a quartet of bottles with the characteristics of an established, noble family.

● *Sainsbury's four "rare jewels"*
Designer: *Nicole Clément-Weiss and Richard Ward*
Art Director: *Richard Ward*
Calligrapher: *Richard Ward*

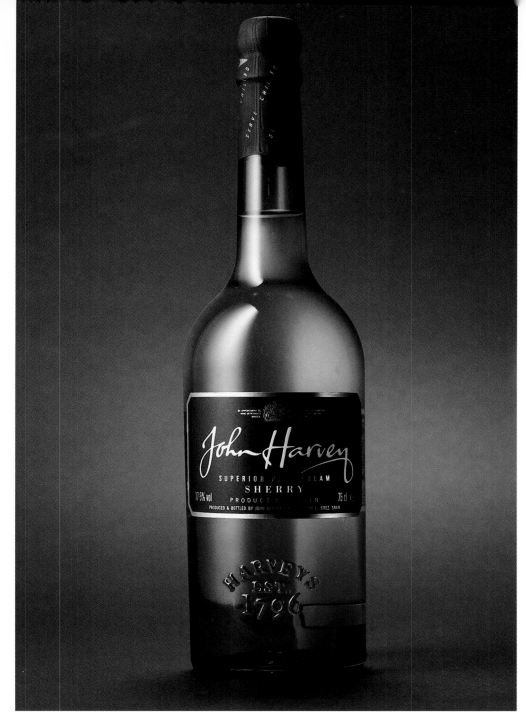

J ohn Harvey sherry was originally launched with a pack
design which failed to perform
on the shelf and remained anonymous and lacking in in-store
presence.

Kyte & Company's task was to try
to retain whatever integrity the
original pack still had - essentially
the bottle shape and the colour of
the glass - tackle the problems of
the heritage and parentage of the
brand, and give it more in-store
presence.

The design solution centres
on the authenticity of the John
Harvey signature with the Harvey's
endorsement moulded into
the glass.

● *Added character for a sherry*
from John Harvey & Sons Limited
Designer: *Ray Kyte*
Art Director: *Ray Kyte*
Calligrapher: *Ruth Rowland*

Brewer Riddiford

Whitbread's brief to Brewer Riddiford was to create a brand identity which would give Murphy's Irish Stout - their "draught in a can" - a more than fighting chance against the market leader, Guinness Draught.

Research showed that Murphy's was already particularly successful with younger people who tend to congregate in trendy pubs and bars dominated by lager sales.

Thus the first task for the designers was to make the can attractive to people with no interest in the imagery of "real ale".

Cream was used as the main pack colour, to lighten its image and avoid the dark or black visual clichés associated with stout and to hint at the creaminess of the product within.

The can's decoration was deliberately kept uncluttered, again to avoid traditional ale signals. The logo was removed from its original red roundel, and a new banner shape was generated with black and cream lettering. To bring colour and freshness to the pack, the green hops and background were kept from the original logo, in an adapted form. Finally, the contours of the logo were heavily indented, to compensate for the flattening effect introduced by the curvature of the can.

● *Uncluttered design for Whitbread's Murphy's Irish Stout*
Designer: *John Wynne*
Art Director: *John Brewer*
Photographer: *Chris Knaggs*

IT HAS ALWAYS been presumed that X means strength but, in fact, the very strongest premium liquids have always been marked with a K. If then you want the ultimate in Cider quality and strength look for this K

275 ml
No. 062089

K

*"The Ultimate in quality
and strength"*

8.4% vol.

C I D E R

● *The ultimate cider from Showerings*
Designer: *Glenn Tutssell*
Art Director: *Glenn Tutssell*

● **Michael Peters Limited**

I n the drinks industry it has always been presumed that X stands for strength but, in fact, the very strongest premium liquids have always been marked with a K.

Showerings' brief to Michael Peters was to design a pack structure and surface graphics which would reflect the ultimate in cider strength and quality.

The black bottle evokes the feeling of alcoholic strength. The minimal graphics convey the understated character. A thick strip of type contains all the product story.

Ziggurat Design Consultants

Wanting to build on their success in crossover marketing by introducing a new super-premium cider to compete with premium bottled lagers, Taunton Cider briefed Ziggurat on the launch of Brody Cider.

Rather than simply feature the product's strength, the designers have created a brand invested with layers of mystique and apparent history.

The clear glass and exceptionally clean lines of the antique bottle make heroes of the colour and clarity of the drink itself.

The bottle shape is an ideal vehicle for the discrete credentials of the Jamestown Brewing Company, the signature of James Brody and the confident character of the logo. Together, these features create an intriguing image for the badge-conscious male drinker, projecting the idea that this is a quality drink first, and a cider second.

- *Taunton Cider's new
Brody premium brand*
Designer: *Monica Jones*
Art Directors: *Bernard Gormley
and David Wombwell*

● *Taunton Cider's new*
Red Rock brand
Designer: *Paul Davies*
Art Director: *Bernard Gormley*

● **Ziggurat Design Consultants**

By turning its back on the old image of cider, Red Rock has been the first brand to appeal successfully to an enormous new market - the "session" lager drinker. For Taunton Cider, its introduction has been "the most successful cider launch of the last decade".

Ziggurat were given strategic responsibility at the outset for positioning the brand and devising its name, its bottle shape, label design and bar mount. Rather than present it as just another cider, they created a new brand tailor-made for the young male drinker.

The name cuts loose from country yokel associations, and starts afresh. It feels easy to ask for in a pub or bar and, with its mountain and sunburst device, seems even faintly exotic.

Yet it is not simply the graphics which set it apart from other ciders. The compact, stubby bottle has a distinct masculinity, while the inverted triangle of the bar mount gives Red Rock an eye-catching presence in a crowded market.

Light & Coley

L ight & Coley's brief from
Courage was to develop a new
image for their Directors Bitter, a
product aimed at discerning bitter
drinkers known to be prepared to
pay a little more for a premium
product.

  Their solution was to develop a
graphic style which does not follow
the traditional image of beer can
packaging but which, through its
understated character, is more akin
to wine bottle labelling and cigar
packaging.

• *A new departure for Courage's*
premium bitter
Designer: *Chris Abrahams*
Art Director: *Laurie Light*

● **Baker Jażdżewski Limited**

Webster's Yorkshire Bitter, acquired by Courage in 1991, is the third-best selling bitter brand in the UK.

The key communication elements in Courage's design brief were inherent in the brand's values as a product. It's a bitter to be supped and savoured rather than quaffed. Webster's is also canned using a unique filling technique which guarantees draught bitter qualities once the beer is poured into a glass. The brand has a fundamental "Yorkshireness" which the new design would also have to enhance.

The solution is an evolution of the original can design created by Baker Jażdżewski, and is clearly recognisable by Webster's brand loyalists through its basic black and cream colourways and its familiar red and white brand banner.

However, this design features a new illustration of a rural Pennine waterfall, introduced to reinforce the authenticity of the brand's Yorkshire origins (the beer is brewed with pure Pennine water), and focuses on the product's superior quality, which is strongly branded for maximum impact.

In a clear break with tradition, the can now has two different faces, with the back of the can given over to a full product story and serving instructions. This strengthens the message of draught quality which appears on the front.

● *Webster's evolution for*
Courage Brewing Limited
Designer: *Andrzej Jażdżewski*
Art Director: *Andrzej Jażdżewski*
Illustrator: *Kim Lane*

Design Bridge UK Limited

As one of South Wales' oldest breweries, the majority of Brains' tied houses are in and around the Cardiff area.

Until recently, most of the company's output was sold on tap. Then, in 1985, the brewery began to look for ways to promote sales of take-home beers, initially offering Brains Dark and Brains Bitter in cans.

In 1989 Brains decided to redesign their existing packs.

Design Bridge drew their inspiration for this project from Cardiff itself. The city and its surrounding area form one of the great industrial and commercial complexes of the nineteenth century. Its rich heritage includes the docks, a fine City Hall, the Great Western Railway, rugby football and, of course, Brains Brewery.

The resultant quartered pattern on the can derives its basic shape from traditional pub signs, although many Welsh rugby players and supports might beg to differ!

● *History influenced the design for Brains' beers*
Designer: *Steve Elliott*
Art Director: *Rod Petrie*

● Darrell Ireland

The design objective for Watney Mann centred on the development of a highly distinctive brand identity for their Armstrong's Pure Malt Scottish ale, which could then be effectively marketed as an export to Italy.

The brand name was developed to endorse the strength of the product, while the label shape was created to mirror the recent history of traditional label design. Complementing these design factors is a detailed illustration depicting a kilted Scottish hammer-thrower practising on a lonely hill-side.

The complete design gives the product a strong presence on store shelves, and a solidly traditional image suggesting a drink ready to supply sound fortification to any purchaser.

● *A new Scottish ale for export to Italy by Watney Mann*
Designers: *Darrell Ireland and Trung Tang*
Art Director: *Darrell Ireland*
Illustrator: *David Hopkins*

Ziggurat Design Consultants

To celebrate its 250 years in the brewing business, Whitbread commissioned 65,000 pints of the finest ale it could brew, and asked Ziggurat to develop the packaging for it.

Because such a fine and complex ale could only be produced with 1990s' technology, the designers were briefed to create a pack which would give a contemporary expression to 250 years of brewing craft and experience, rather than a simply nostalgic or historic pack.

The design began with a commemorative bottle. Instead of a straightforward label, an all-over, individually numbered wrap was adopted, to protect the beer from the light. This carries a brief history of Whitbread's and the story of the special brew on its reverse.

The beer will not reach its full maturity for another 15-20 years. To provide additional protection each bottle is packed with wood straw in a wooden box.

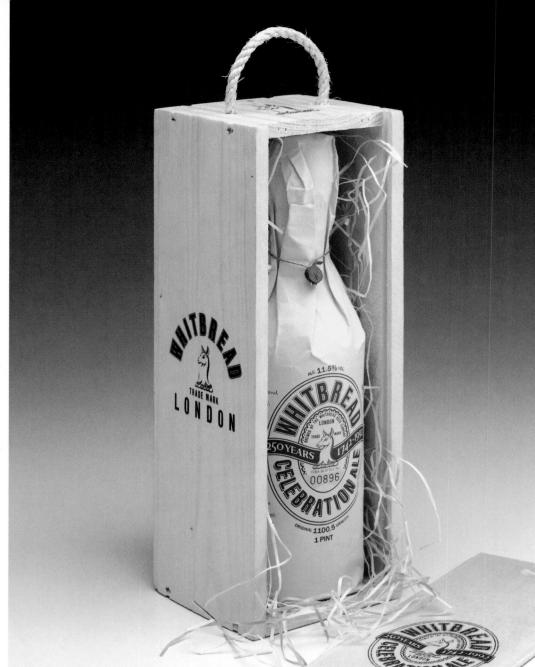

● *Commemorating Whitbread's*
250 years as brewing experts
Designer: *Paul Davies*
Art Director: *David Wombwell*

● *Shakespearean themes for*
  Whitbread's Flowers Original
  Designer: *John Wynne*
  Art Director: *John Brewer*
  Photographer: *Chris Knaggs*

● Brewer Riddiford

Whitbread's brief to Brewer Riddiford called for the development of the Flowers' Shakespeare identity across all the existing Flowers products, followed by the introduction of a can for Flowers Original Strong Ale.

The first part of this project involved strengthening the brewery's traditional links with Stratford-on-Avon by enhancing the existing Shakespeare character.

Subsequently, Shakespeare was introduced into the Flowers Original Strong Ale branding and incorporated into the designs for Flowers Original's first appearance in a can.

The established type of "Flowers Original" was used to create a rounded shape encircling the central Shakespeare figure.

The words "Strong Ale" also had to be accentuated, without letting them disturb the legibility of "Flowers Original". A red key-line achieves the right emphasis, while smaller type and a central position help avoid any cluttering of the main part of the brand name.

The exact typeface for Flowers Original was specially designed to give it a more traditional quality - sympathetic to real ale drinkers - and to distance it from any hint of trendy cult lager signals.

Elmwood Design Limited

Scorpion Dry is a new dry lager from Vaux Breweries. Dry lagers presently constitute a small but exclusive niche in the UK beer market. As such, the style of their packaging tends to be distinct from the embellished look of traditional premium lagers.

Scorpion Dry's minimalist graphics reflect this, with gold being used to reinforce the hot, arid desert imagery of the brand's name, which Elmwood also created. The typestyle is essentially strong and masculine, in keeping the market's known image.

- *Designs for Vaux Breweries' new dry lager*
  Designer: *Gary Swindell*
  Art Director: *Gary Swindell*

● **Lewis Moberly**

Zeiss is a premium lager from
Bass. It is 8% proof and made
with champagne yeast to give it a
distinctive flavour. In a market
flooded with 'me too' products,
Zeiss is a genuinely different lager.
The packaging aims to reflect this.
The bottle features a punt - which
evokes a champagne bottle - with
graphics screened directly onto
etched dark green glass. The black
foil collar aims to reinforce the
lager's unique champagne
character.

● *A champagne-style image*
for Bass's Zeiss lager
Designer: *David Beard*
Art Director: *Mary Lewis*

● *Simple style for Tooheys from*
Whitbread Breweries
Designer: *Chris Halton*
Art Director: *Ian Ritchie*

● Jones Knowles Ritchie

Tooheys is an Australian pre-mium strength lager and the brand leader in New South Wales.

Imported into the UK by Whit-bread, it has been positioned as an easy going "up" brand for male session drinking.

Jones Knowles Ritchie's surface designs for Tooheys use simple, bold typography balanced with a two-tone silver base colour to achieve an unpretentious appeal while still projecting the idea of a strong, premium product.

The net effect gives the cans a great deal of impact on the busy shelves of off-licences and supermarkets.

● **Darrell Ireland**

Despite its relative success as a brand, Holsten Export lager was considered by its marketing team to lack authority, authenticity and any real presence when placed alongside its immediate competitors. Yet the product is one of the best on the market, regularly enjoyed by a devoted following.

The solution to this presentational problem was not drastic surgery, which could have meant the alienation of many loyal customers, but a gentle re-working of all the prominent elements within the existing design, refining and harmonising them until they represented one essential unit with the Holsten shield.

The silver stripe was kept, although widened, from the original design; the brewing heritage was clarified; the grey-brown background was introduced - after much experimentation and testing - to enhance the central design without distracting from the main image. Finally, the copy describing the contents was given more prominence and enhanced by a small line illustration of hops and barley which attracts the eye to the German lager producer's claim that only four key ingredients, together with centuries of brewing knowledge, go into the making of this purest of lagers.

● *Refining a well-known image*
for Watney Mann
Designer: *Darrell Ireland*
Art Director: *Darrell Ireland*

Michael Peters Limited

Carling Extra Dry is a strong lager aimed at the younger, style-conscious drinker. Brewed with a fuller fermentation, it has a distinctively strong, dry, refreshing flavour.

This is reflected in the pack design, which features a specially created crest designed to give the lager authenticity and immediate heritage. The crest appears subtly as a shiny silver image against a matt silver background.

The brand's links with its parent are achieved through the use of a black panel bearing the brand name, which has a touch of red to give warmth to the words "Extra Dry".

The surface graphics were deliberately designed to enhance the unusual tulip-shaped can and create maximum shelf impact.

● *Bass's Carling Extra Dry lager*
Designer: *Garrick Hamm*
Art Director: *Glenn Tutssel*
Illustrator: *Peter Horridge*

● **Michael Peters Limited**

I n its native Italy, Nastro Azzuro is the only nationally produced beer in the premium sector, and the only brand asked for by name. However, its success has been confined to hotel, retail and catering outlets, while its Peroni corporate endorsement has caused confusion between it and its mainstream sister brand, Birra Peroni.

The main task for Michael Peters was to consolidate Nastro Azzuro's overall leadership of the premium sector of the market and improve its position in the off licence trade.

The designers' aim was to take an evolutionary step away from the current design and achieve a change of direction while still retaining the positive elements of the old identity.

Research among consumers showed the extent and nature of what was desirable, thus pointing the way to the optimum solution.

The final design features a clean, white background for a refreshing premium appearance with the brand name re-drawn to incorporate a ribbon ("nastro" in Italian) within the letter "A". The Peroni endorsement has been reduced in importance and removed from the ribbon device. It and a refined blue ribbon under the brand name hold together the key elements of the new identity.

● *Tesco Stores' new French lager*
Designers: *Sean Langford*
and Tony Enoch
Art Director: *Gerard O'Dwyer*
Photographer: *David Gill*

● The London Design Partnership

Responding to the increasing consumer interest in more exotic and international beers, and keen to secure its own share of this market, Tesco launched its own Biére d'Alsace with brand new packaging from The London Design Partnership.

The French flag was used as a backdrop to the design, to convey both the product's strong association with France and its premium quality as a lager.

The flag was photographed, rather than illustrated, to give the packs a contemporary, fresh feel.

Davies Hall

S ainsbury's Biére de Garde is a premium French ale brewed at Bénifontaine in the Nord-Pas de Calais region where brewing traditions date back to the Middle Ages. Biére de Garde retains the traditional French long-necked bottle and cork stopper.

Davies Hall's brief was to create a strong and credible brand identity for the beer. The cockerel motif is reminiscent of poster-style French graphics, and reinforces the provenance of the ale. Traditionally earthy colours reflect the beer's full flavour and rich amber colour. The use of gold emphasises the product's quality. The brand identity is rich and striking and successfully combines an expression of quality and a strong shelf presence.

A new beer from Sainsbury's
Designer: *Steve Davies*
Art Director: *Steve Davies*
Illustrator: *Steve Davies*

Light & Coley

In a new but business-related departure for them, Bryant & May - the UK's leading match manufacturer - were planning to break into the cigarette paper market with the launch of a Swan brand of hand rolling papers.

Light & Coley were briefed to develop packaging designs which would appeal to the specific target market of hand rolling smokers.

The design deliberately reflects the traditional craft aspirations of such smokers, as well as having an appeal to younger people through its image of "contemporary nostalgia".

Almost the entire design was hand-drawn. The borders were developed from original wood-cut designs, the illustrative work was drawn to harmonise with the concept, and the brand's namestyle was similarly hand crafted.

● *A brand new departure*
  for Bryant & May
  Designer: *Cindy Scott*
  Art Director: *Alan Coley*

Raymond Loewy International

The marketing concept for Star cigarettes, developed by Philip Morris-FTR and Sulzer & Sulzer Advertising, envisaged a collection of different packs which would change periodically to appeal to fashion and style conscious young consumers in the Swiss market.

The first pack commemorated the fall of the Berlin Wall, with the brand name treated as a tag on the Wall itself.

The second pack is based on the work of the English illustrator, Dave Westwood, who was asked to adapt one of his futuristic images which, with its architectural overtones, then formed the basis for the design.

New work for Philip Morris[1]
Star Cigarettes
Designer: *Niall Monro*
Art Director: *Thomas R. Riedel*
Illustrator: *Dave Westwood*

Ziggurat Design Consultants

Before the re-design of this packaging, Cortez was already Scandinavia's leading cigar brand. However, the Swedish Tobacco Group's international ambitions called for a clearer, more cohesive identity to pull together a range of different cigars and varying pack sizes.

Ziggurat's new approach centres on the visual device used on the original cigarillos pack while re-inforcing the brand name in a consistent way across the extended range.

The packs' background colours and typographic treatments convey an air of quality which is carried through in the copy which describes each product.

● *Quality for Frans Suell Cigars*
Designers: *Monica Jones and Paul Davies*
Art Director: *David Wombwell*
Illustrator: *Jim Gibson*

TOBACCO SERIOUSLY DAMAGES HEALTH

● *Out of the ordinary design*
for Gallaher Limited
Designers: *Martin Lewsley*
and Nigel Tudman
Art Director: *Laurie Light*
Illustrator: *Mark Longworth*

● **Light & Coley**

Following intensive research which highlighted an opportunity for a new brand in the premium sector of its market, Gallaher - one of the UK's leading tobacco companies - recently introduced "Eclipse", its first 120mm cigarette.

The perceived need was for a brand which would be "out of the ordinary" and "for that special occasion, distinct from the everyday humdrum routine of life".

It was this need to be different and individualistic which generated an initial series of names and pack designs, all of which had to be identifiably different to the more uniform, structured packs already on the market.

Light & Coley's response to the brief is a radical departure from the usual kind of cigarette pack design. As an occasional cigarette and an "accessory", there is nothing else quite like it on the market today.

ng **NOW** · I

ckaging **NOW** · British packag

NOW · British packaging

British pac

· B

NOW · British packaging **NOW** ·

ish pac

● **Cosmetic and Medical Products**

In this section we feature cosmetic and beauty products, toiletries and sun-tan lotions and some comparatively mundane medical products, all of which have been given striking personalities by their packaging designers.

The London Design Partnership

The brief for the packaging for this range of toiletries from Laura Ashley centred on the need to communicate the quintessential "Englishness" associated with the company and its products.

The "No 1" fabric was one of Laura Ashley's favourites. It was thus an obvious choice as a motif for the "No 1" parfum and eau de toilet.

The combination of the fabric pattern and this elegant typography conveys the essence and mood of Laura Ashley's design philosophy.

Laura Ashley's new
range of toiletries
Designer: *Johanna Grellier*
Art Director: *Gerard O'Dwyer*

A new departure for
Crabtree & Evelyn's "Gardenia"
Designers: *Kay Winstanley*
and Peter Windett
Art Director: *Peter Windett*
Photographer: *Clay Perry*

Peter Windett & Associates

The brief for this project was to create the packaging for a range of luxury toiletries scented with gardenia blossom. The packaging had to reflect the attributes of the scent and the source flower, and thus convey the purity of the bloom, its rare, exotic nature, and the luxury of the resultant product.

The packaging was a new departure for Crabtree & Evelyn, who have been known until now for designs based on botanical illustrations.

The image for this range is photographic. Sections from a single shot of gardenia flowers and leaves by Clay Perry were used to create a flow of blossom images across the various shapes and size of packages in the range. The leaves are dark and glossy, setting off the short-lived and rare beauty of the gardenia's waxy, white flowers.

The silver type is crisp and simple, apart from the "Gardenia" logo which, with its elaborate swashes, gives the pack impact and stamps it with a classic yet contemporary image.

● *A non-macho image*
for Parfums Icardi Egan
Designers: *Peter Kay, Mary Lewis*
and Margaret Nolan
Art Director: *Mary Lewis*
Photographer: *Robin Broadbent*

● **Lewis Moberly**

Journey is a mass market male fragrance which breaks new ground by moving away from the generally macho overtones of its competitors towards a stronger expression of individuality and sensitivity. It aims to present the consumer with a voyage of discovery; an experience reflected through the style and pace of the packaging.

Both the bottle and the outer carton offer layers of intrigue, mystery and revelation.

The unique frosted aquamarine bottle is slim and cool to the touch, with a distinctive split profile and "drill-hole" embossed detailing which adds to the tactile and visual experience offered by the product. The black and white graphics are deliberately clear and simple.

The carton is unusual in what is a generally bland sector of the market. It is formed by two sections which slide apart to reveal the fragrance bottle within. The design of this was as carefully considered as that for the bottle, with the aim of making the carton a desirable thing to keep.

● **Pentagram Design Limited**

S hiseido, the world's third largest cosmetics manufacturer, commissioned Pentagram to design the packaging for Trendy, a new collection of men's toiletries aimed at the Japanese youth market.

Projecting an up-to-date image, Pentagram's design incorporates graphic elements found in current Japanese youth culture. A collage combines symbols and letters (based on the brand name Trendy) with bright day-glo colours, while the bottles have been given exaggerated, rippled shoulders and bright coloured plastic triangles which extend from the caps. The result reflects the break with tradition which is found in the Japanese youth movement.

● *Youth movement themes*
for Shiseido
Designers: *Kenneth Grange*
and Mervyn Kurlansky
Art Director: *Mervyn Kurlansky*

● *Extra Performance for*
Germaine de Capuccini
Designer: *Kathy Miller*
Art Director: *Kathy Miller*
Photographer: *David Harrison*

● **Miller Sutherland**

As the brand leader in the Spanish skincare/salon treatment market, Germaine de Capuccini's brief to Miller Sutherland was simple: to redesign the company's identity and introduce a range of products which would be the catalyst for the company's entry into the kind of international markets where they would be competing with global brands such as Clinique and Shiseido.

Extra Performance is the first line in a new range of luxury products for the world.

The concept for this luxury range centres on the use of abstracted photography to express the product's benefits. This in itself is a new and distinctive approach in this particular market.

Extra Performance is a collection of treatments for dehydrated and dry skins, so moisturising and nourishing are easily seen as their key benefits. The colours of the pack are in

sympathy with water imagery while the use of strong colours inside the pack not only provides another layer of interest, but also - as with Germaine de Capuccini's Specialist Range - introduces an element of surprise into the product's personality.

*A new range for the Spanish
leaf, Germaine de Capuccini*
Designer: *Kathy Miller*
Art Director: *Kathy Miller*

● **Miller Sutherland**

Miller Sutherland were
commissioned to assist in a
major rationalisation of the products
of Germaine de Capuccini, the brand
leader in the Spanish skin care/salon
treatment market.

This initial project resulted in the
development of the range of
specialist treatment lines seen here.

The Specialist Range includes
products which contain ingredients
such as royal jelly, herbal extracts,

minerals and ginseng. The packaging
design symbolises these special
ingredients through the use of a
blind embossed illustration. The
unusual use of soft feminine colours
on the pack's exterior contrasts
sharply with the strong colours inside
and creates an element of surprise:
something with an extra something
without being over packaged. The
bottle, jar and tottle for the range
were also designed by Kathy Miller,
who was looking for simplicity,
elegance and an emphasis on how

the product would feel in the hand.

The range has proved so successful
for Germaine de Capuccini that it
has opened up new markets for the
company throughout America and
Europe.

Trickett & Webb Limited

John Frieda first commissioned Trickett & Webb to produce pack designs for a range of haircare products launched to coincide with the opening of his salon in the Ritz Hotel, London.

In the early days, the small production volumes made exclusive hand-finished packs possible. With a corporate identity based on John Frieda's signature, the packs were printed using letterpress techniques to achieve the richness of quality the designers wanted. It was even possible for each one to be hand sealed in its own cellophane wrapper. Press information packs and carrier bags were also created, carrying the identity beyond the immediate confines of the Ritz.

The first range of products was so successful that it was soon extended and quickly on sale in various up-market department stores.

The range shown here is sold worldwide in packs which, though they are now produced in much greater numbers using mass production methods, still have the same style and sophistication of the initial designs.

At the outset, John Frieda had said he wanted his products to "look good enough to eat".

Even now, in their second generation, they have lost nothing of that quality.

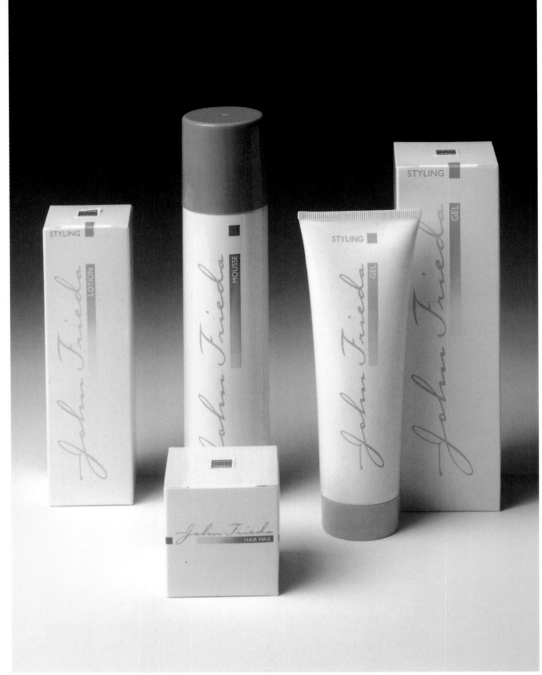

Simple sophistication for John Frieda's haircare range
Designers: *Fiona Skelsey, Lynn Trickett and Brian Webb*
Art Directors: *Lynn Trickett and Brian Webb*

S cimetics' cosmetic and healthcare products are sold through multi-level marketing into a comparatively small market.

As scientifically based products with medical formulations, the items in the range are packed in standard containers such as pill boxes, jars, bottles and tubes.

Working within a limited budget, the designers were faced with the task of conveying the products' medical attributes in a way which would work in harmony with an image of cleanliness and beauty.

The solution lies in the opalescent colouring, which gives many of the packs a pearly quality, and in an utterly simple typographic styling which features a small cross evocative of medicine and healing.

Several of the products are marketed with instructional literature which carries the identity right through the range.

• *Clinical simplicity for*
Scimetics Limited
Designers: *Avril Broadley,*
Lynn Trickett and Brian Webb
Art Directors: *Lynn Trickett*
and Brian Webb

Lewis Moberly

Yves Rocher's Les Huiles Essentielles aromatherapy oils contain highly concentrated plant essences. The fragrances in the range include lavender, pine, rosemary and cyprus. Lewis Moberly's packaging aims to convey the natural efficacy of the plants and the soothing qualities of aromatherapy. The logo projects an elegant style and, in the way it extends right round the bottle, takes the eye around the form thus creating a tactile dialogue with the consumer. Similarly, the disappearing typography on the carton invites the consumer to turn the pack to read about the products' key benefits.

● *Conveying the essence of natural goodness for Yves Rocher's Les Huiles Essentielles*
Designer: *Lucilla Scrimgeour*
Art Director: *Mary Lewis*
Illustrator: *Lucilla Scrimgeour*

● *Breaking new ground with*
Tesco's soap designs
Designer: *Sean Langford*
Art Director: *Gerard O'Dwyer*
Photographer: *Nick Georghiou*

● **The London Design Partnership**

T esco's brief for this project called for a range of packaging for a premium collection of glycerine soaps with fruit fragrances.

The designers' response breaks new ground in this market by featuring a still-life photographic image in the style of a time-worn oil painting with carefully chosen classic type faces.

The success of the project depended on the creation of a unique design which would work in a market crowded with homogeneity.

● Klaus Wuttke & Partners

W hen Cussons were planning
the launch of the UK's first
unisex shower gel, they involved
designers Klaus Wuttke & Partners in
every aspect of the product's
development.

Thus it was possible for everything
from the brand name to the product
colour, the surface graphics and the
shape of the bottle to be harmonised
to project the desired brand image.

The designers developed a dra-
matically different concept for
AquaSpa, including an ergonomically
attractive rounded container whose
shape and classic proportions echo
the purity and simplicity of the
product.

The clip on/clip off cap locks onto
the bottom of the pack for easy use,
and incorporates a highly functional,
integral, hinged hook which ensures
that the bottle always hangs verti-
cally.

The bottle is made of a clear,
slightly tinted PET material which
enhances the crystal clarity of the
gel inside. The simple surface design
has an unambiguous, uni-sex appeal.

The designers' complete involve-
ment in this project from start to
finish has resulted in a product with
a strong brand identity which works
well in the crowded cosmetics
market.

● *A fresh design for Elida Gibbs*
  SR toothpaste
  Designer: *Ian Delaney*
  Art Director: *Ian Grindle*

● **Minale, Tattersfield & Partners**

Despite its 50-year history in the market - or perhaps because of it - Gibbs SR toothpaste was being severely challenged by increasing competition from own brand products.

Minale Tattersfield's brief called for the retention of some of the traditional SR properties, such as the powerful livery of red, white and blue, but yet for a solution which would give the product much more impact on supermarket and pharmacy shelves.

The new design gives a crisp, uncluttered look to both the tube and the carton by capitalising on SR's properties - ice, mountains and snow - whose inherent notions of freshness, strength and health apply as much today as they did in 1955 when the product was first advertised on television.

The mountain skyline is in marked contrast to the generally abstract nature of much toothpaste pack design, and thus gives SR an unmistakable identity. The echoes in the mountains of a row of gleaming white teeth are far from unintentional.

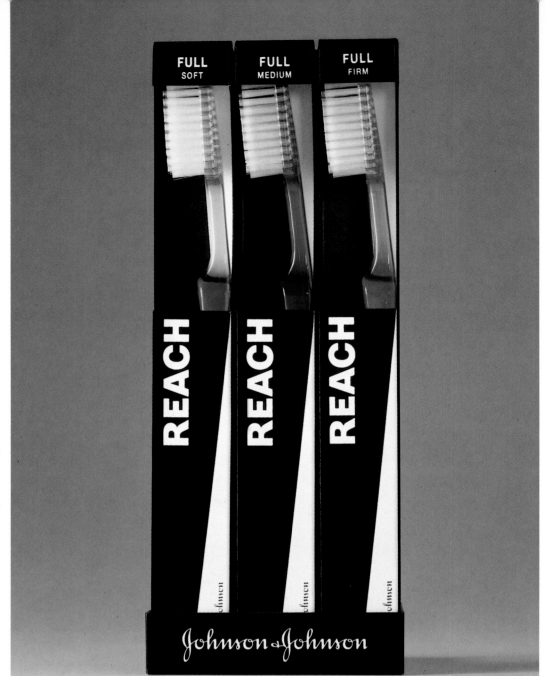

Lewis Moberly

The designers' brief for this project was to strengthen the brand's presence on the shelf and further emphasise the "therapeutic but accessible" promise of the product.

As an individualistic brand in a very busy sector, Reach is defiantly black, itself unusual in dental hygiene, and single minded in its stance. Its well-known property is its angled head.

The packaging is uncompromisingly black and white with a design which creates a strong image on the shelf when the product is repeated as part of a display.

The design also communicates authority and superiority on the one hand, and has a young, mass market appeal on the other.

A new design for
Johnson & Johnson's toothbrush
Designers: Ann Marshall
and Mary Lewis
Art Director: Mary Lewis

● *A more competitive image*
  for Sainsbury's toothpaste
  Designer: *Nicole Clément-Weiss*
  Art Director: *Richard Ward*

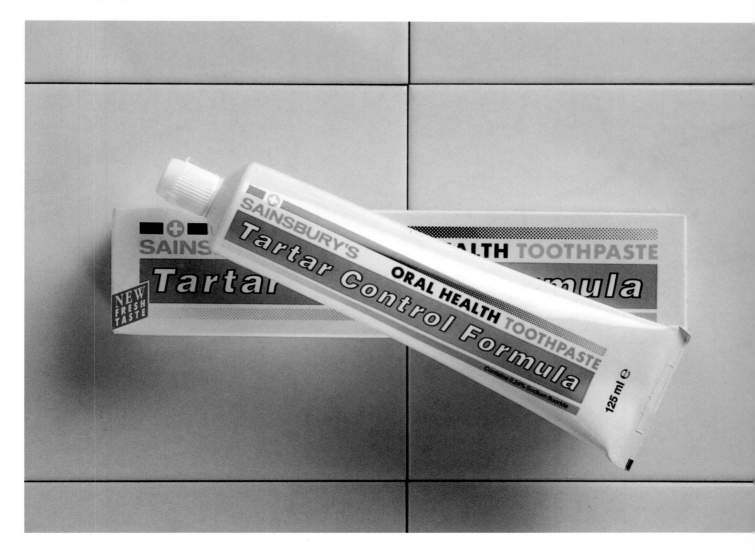

● **The Team**

Competition in the toothpaste market is fierce. This own-label product was re-designed for Sainsbury's to portray a stronger image in order to compete more directly with the tartar control brand leaders.

The use of gold was important because consumers associate it with tartar control products. The overall image of the packaging had to reflect the clinical nature and efficacy of the product, and yet still retain the Sainsbury's corporate logo and typestyle developed for oral health products.

● *Sunny designs for Safeway plc*
Designer: *Philip Carter*
Art Director: *Philip Carter*

● **Carter Wong**

The Safeway brief to Carter Wong was to produce designs for a new, own-label range of suntan lotions.

The key messages which the packs were expected to communicate were the products' efficacy and their suitability for family use.

Carter Wong's clean and uncomplicated graphic style successfully meets these objectives while still capturing some of the fun and enjoyment of holidays and leisure time spent in the sun.

New sun-care designs for Tesco
Designer: *Chen Tsoi*
Art Director: *Chen Tsoi*
Illustrator: *Lawrence Partridge*

● **Chen Tsoi Design**

One of the most important things about buying any sun-care product is its Sun Protection Factor (SPF).

It was this which was borne in mind when the designers tackled the brief for the Tesco range of sun-care products. The SPF number is featured boldly as part of the illustration, flanked by a gold-foiled sun which is positioned to reflect the particular sun strength each product is designed to protect against.

This design concept has been used across Tesco's extensive range of products, including Water-Resistant versions and After-Sun Lotions.

● *Inspired new ideas for*
Roche's Valderma range
Designers: *Ian Grindle*
and Liz Knight
Art Director: *Ian Grindle*

● Minale, Tattersfield & Partners

Valderma was an ageing brand in an uninspiring market: skin (and more specifically, spot) treatment. Hampered by a lack-lustre image and having to compete with more aggressively marketed brands, it was in need of a major re-think.

The first stage in its revitalisation came when Roche bought the brand in 1990. The two original products - an antibacterial soap and an anti-bacterial cream - were then joined by a third and stronger skin treatment product aimed at the teenage market: Valderma Active Gel.

Armed with this trio of products, Roche brought in Minale Tattersfield to bring the brand up-to-date.

The new design cuts a triangular slice off the top of the vertical square-sectioned pack to create the "V" of Valderma in a contrasting colour. The result is unique, both in colour and shape. The traditional blue associated with skin products has been subtly altered by giving it a tinge of green, and used in combination with a range of contrasting secondary colours: pink for the cream, blue for the soap and a bright yellow for the gel.

The introduction of the pharmaceutical "cross" formed by the two Vs of Valderma adds medical weight to the look of the brand.

● *A new look for medical examination
gloves for ABT Limited*
Designers: *Jim Groark, Joann
Weedon and Nicholas Kendall*
Art Director: *Tor Pettersen*

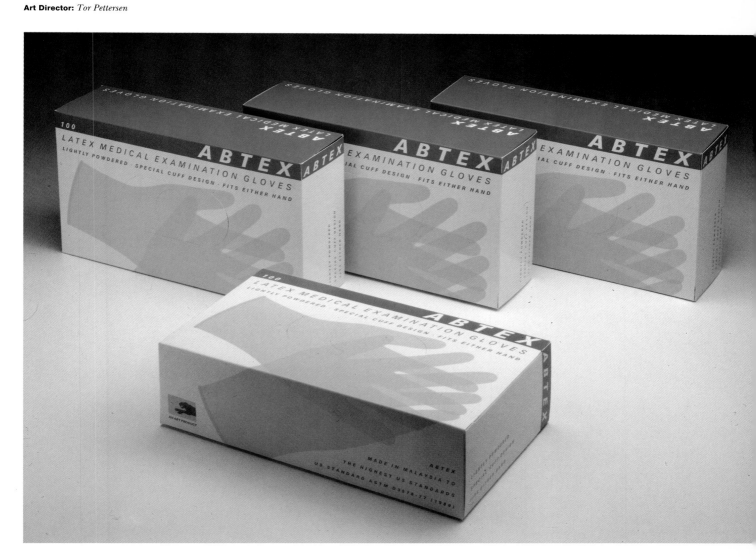

● **Tor Pettersen & Partners**

The market for medical
examination gloves has grown
tremendously during the past
decade, mainly due to the increased
threat of infection from dangerous
viruses such as Hepatitis B and AIDS.
  In the USA, sales have increased
from a quarter-of-a-billion units ten
years ago to more than ten billion
units today.
  Tor Pettersen & Partners were
commissioned by ABT to conduct

qualitative market research in the
USA and the UK, and to name and
create packaging for their range of
medical examination gloves.

NOW • British
British packaging NOW •
NOW • British
NOW • British packaging NOW •
NOW •

● Household Goods

Imaginative, attractive packaging design is not confined to luxury goods or high quality foods. As the examples in this section show, it is just as important in the kitchenware, pet food and household goods markets.

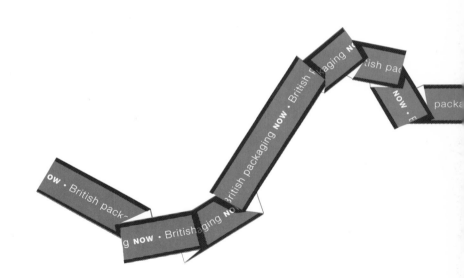

Minale, Tattersfield & Partners

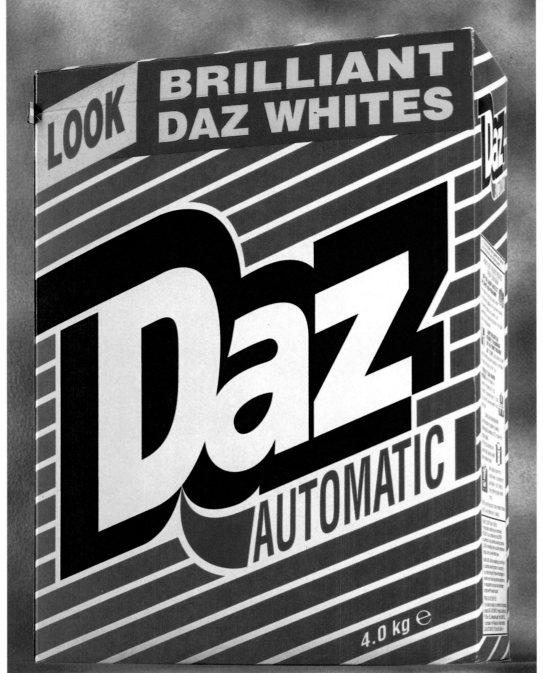

Daz Ultra is the new concentrated version of the famous blue whitener. As a brand with a tradition of service to millions of British housewives, Daz has been a market leader for nearly 40 years. With this in mind, it was important that, in designing the Daz Ultra pack, many of Daz's well-earned values should be retained.

However, despite the request that Minale Tattersfield's work should be evolutionary rather than revolutionary, the designers changed every single element of the pack, injecting a marked degree of modernity into it by using brighter, more fluorescent colours and simplifying the logo and its surrounding flashes.

The overall effect is much cleaner, and consequently the branding is much clearer.

- *A clear, clean image for*
Procter & Gamble's Daz Ultra
Designer: *Marcello Minale Jnr*
Art Director: *Ian Grindle*

● *Micro Surf for Lever Brothers*
Designers: *Klaus Wuttke*
and Liz Gutteridge
Art Director: *Klaus Wuttke*
Illustrator: *David Penny*

● **Klaus Wuttke & Partners**

The brief here was to improve Surf's position in an increasingly competitive market through the launch of Surf Micro, and to create a design which would stand out on the shelf and improve Surf's overall image by conveying its modernity and relevance to today's market conditions.

The results of the designers' work speak for themselves.

Only four months after the launch Surf Micro had nearly reached its targets for market share for the full year. Most of the increase had been incremental business for the brand, while the additional distribution gained by Micro Surf has improved the visibility of the parent brand.

● *Designs for a new carpet cleaner*
for Stafford Miller Limited
Designer: *Paul Cilia la Corte*
Art Director: *John Blackburn*
Illustrator: *Brian Sweet*

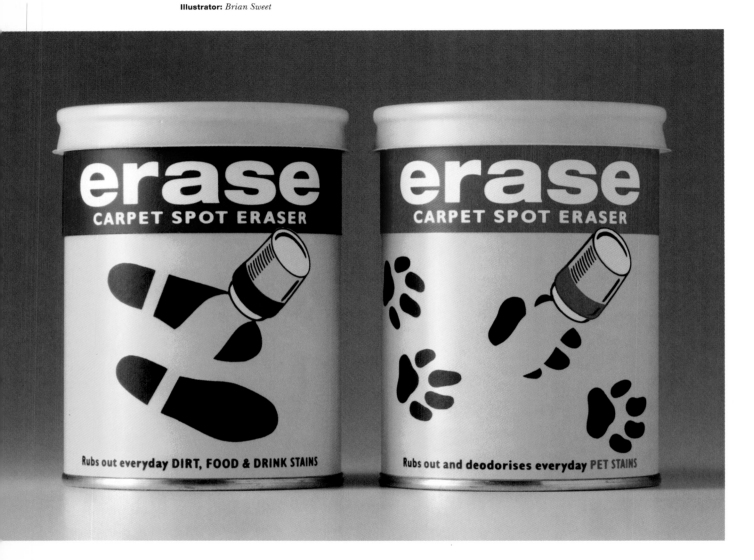

● **Blackburn's Limited**

This bold brand identity with its "road sign type clarity" is designed to prevent confusion between the two formulae for Erase, a new carpet cleaner from America.

The product is contained in a pop-up tube which works as an eraser, rubbing out the dirt in carpets as illustrated on the packaging.

The cartoon-like images help to convey the idea that the product is simple to use, and even fun to work with.

A *brand new product for the*
dynamic Oz Cleaning Company
Designer: *John Blackburn*
Art Director: *John Blackburn*

Blackburn's Limited

Oz is a brand new, dynamic little product from an equally new, dynamic little company.

When Blackburn's got the brief, both "Oz" and the company needed to be seen against established competitive brands from bigger competitive companies.

The green plastic bottle had to be standard, for economic reasons. So Blackburn's created a strong logo which would be compatible with the language of the market, and positioned it prominently on the label.

Overall, the packaging creates a high level of visibility for the product, even when it's displayed on low shelves in supermarkets.

The logostyle design has now been applied to the packaging for three new products - kettle, shower jet and steam iron descalers - as a consistent corporate branding.

● *A simple solution for Tesco's*
Green Choice range
Designers: *Karen Morgan,*
Gareth Howat and Phil Pennington
Art Director: *Shaun Dew*
Illustrations: *Line & Line*

● The Partners

Tesco's Green Choice is a range
of household cleaning products
which tackles a host of differing
environmental concerns such as recycling, CFC-free aerosols, non-
chlorine bleached paper products
and phosphate-free detergents.

The Partners' brief was to develop a
strong brand identity for the product
range which would clearly communicate the environmental message
and be flexible enough to be applied

to a variety of packaging formats. It
would also have to compete successfully with a wide range of established
branded products.

The solution, which presents the
world within a heart, clearly and
simply conveys the environmental
message. The bold and simple
honesty of the design, and the
consistent application of the identity,
ensure a strong shelf presence in an
area where there is a proliferation of
products making environmentally
friendly claims.

● *A strong design for the Co-op's*
Dishwasher Salt
Designer: *Dennis Fenna*
Art Director: *Jack Wrigley*

● **Co-operative Wholesale
Society Limited**

Sales of dishwashers and related products have been growing steadily over the past few years, both nationally and in Co-ops. However, the Co-op's own label products were not increasing their share of the market, and were looking almost monochromatic on the shelf compared with the strong, primary colours of the branded opposition.

Consequently, the design brief called for a radical approach to typography and colour to help the Co-op compete with the major brands. Like many other own label products, the Dishwasher range had to compete with shorter, snappier names; the Co-op's wordiest product title runs to five words compared with five letters on the branded equivalent.

The design makes light of this fact with strong typography giving a branded feel to the longer product titles without the need for sub-branding. Bold, horizontal bars contrast with the fluid shapes and colours of the pots and pans of the background illustration.

The bulk of the range benefitted from five colour litho-printed labels, but the Dishwasher Salt had to work in four colour line flexo, with one colour being cyan. The creation of all the designs in Adobe Illustrator on an Apple Macintosh helped make the final selection of the limited colours much easier than if the project had been carried out conventionally.

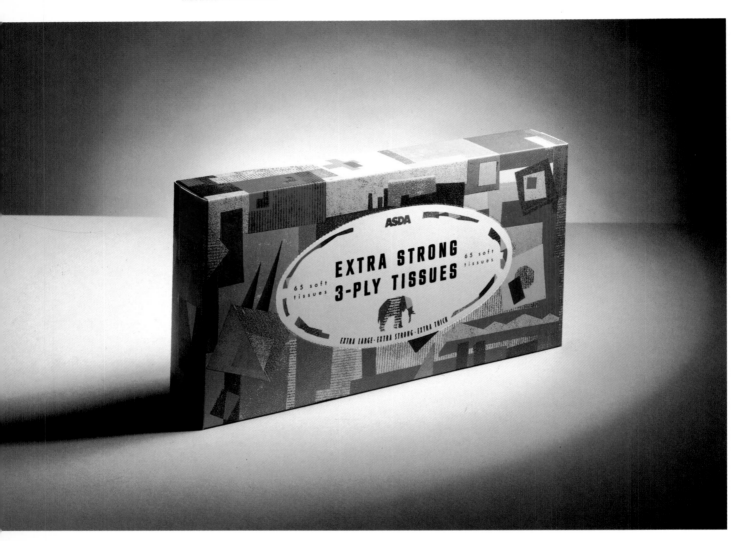

● Elmwood Design Limited

The biggest problem posed by this brief was the need to create a pack which would appeal to both men and women.

Traditionally, "strong" tissues are seen as being very masculine and conservative, with an appearance which reflects this. Nevertheless, the majority of all tissues are bought by women, either on behalf of men or for household use, so it was important not to alienate female customers. At the same time, male users still had to feel comfortable with the pack's appearance, and not feel embarrassed if they wanted to leave it on the parcel shelf of a car or use it in an office. Elmwood's design solution has a striking background made of layers of different paper textures, built up to create a collage effect. Strong colours and hard lines give the product powerful shelf impact and an appeal to male users, while the overall look of the pack allows female users to co-ordinate the pack with household interiors.

The typography and illustration of an elephant all help to reiterate the strength of the product.

● *Recycled tissues for Asda Stores*
Designer: *David Pike*
Art Director: *Glenn Tutssel*
Illustrator: *Malcom Smith*

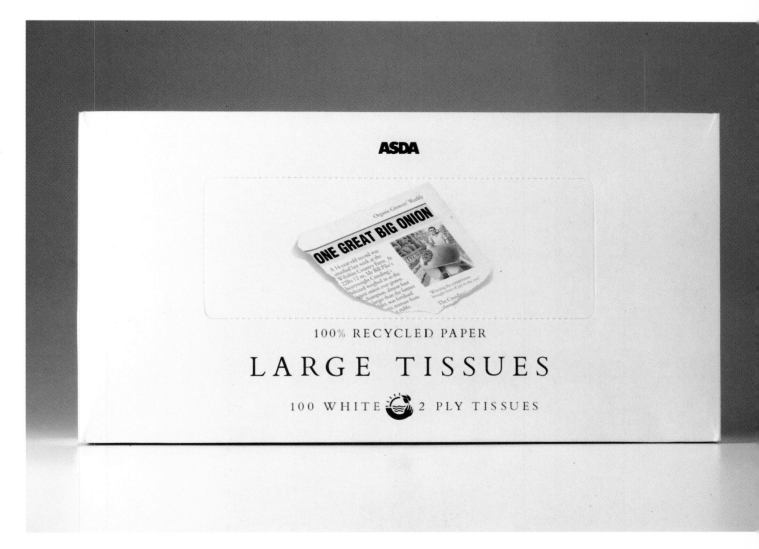

● **Michael Peters Limited**

As one of the items in Asda's range of recycled household tissues, these boxes of large tissues had to emphasise the 100% recycled quality of the product, and have a witty and dynamic presence in the company's stores.

The age-old business of peeling onions bringing tears to one's eyes is well used here, with an illustration of a news item about a giant onion.

● *A new use for crosswords*
  for Asda Stores
  Designer: *David Pike*
  Art Director: *Glenn Tutssel*

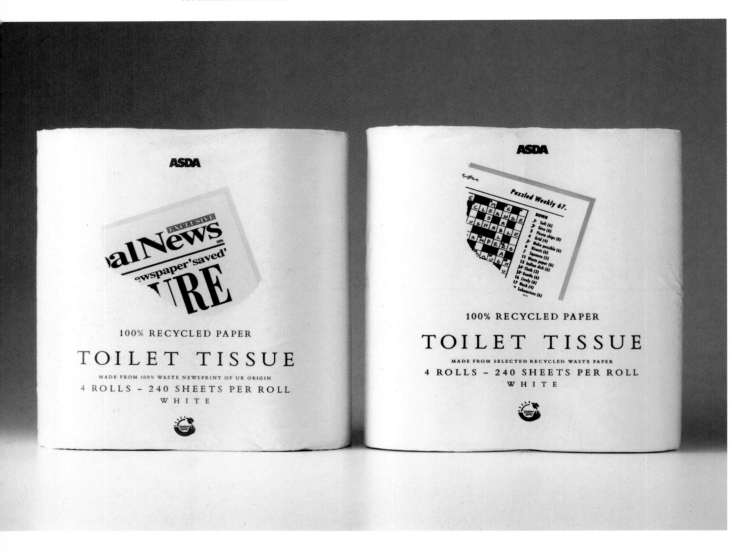

● **Michael Peters Limited**

When Asda launched its own label range of recycled paper tissues for use around the house, the designers were told to emphasise the genuine 100% recycled quality of all the products in the range.

Asda also wanted the products to have a witty appeal to their customers, and a strong identity on the supermarket shelf.

The toilet tissue is made entirely from recycled newspaper. The design plays on this - and on the fact that, in days gone by, newspapers themselves were used as toilet tissue, which meant that crosswords were always available in the lavatory.

● *More tissues from Asda's*
range of household products
Designer: *David Pike*
Art Director: *Glen Tutssel*
Illustrator: *Steve Palmer*

● **Michael Peters Limited**

As another item in Asda's re-cycled household tissues range, these kitchen towels called for a design which emphasises their 100% recycled quality, and has a wit and dynamism which gives them a fight-ing chance on crowded supermarket shelves.

The recipe motif achieves both objectives by showing what often happens in kitchens and by indicat-ing the types of paper - magazines, for example - which have been re-cycled to produce the kitchen roll.

*A simple solution for basic
kitchenware for Boots plc*
Designers: *Alison Tomlin
and Philip Wong*
Art Director: *Philip Wong*

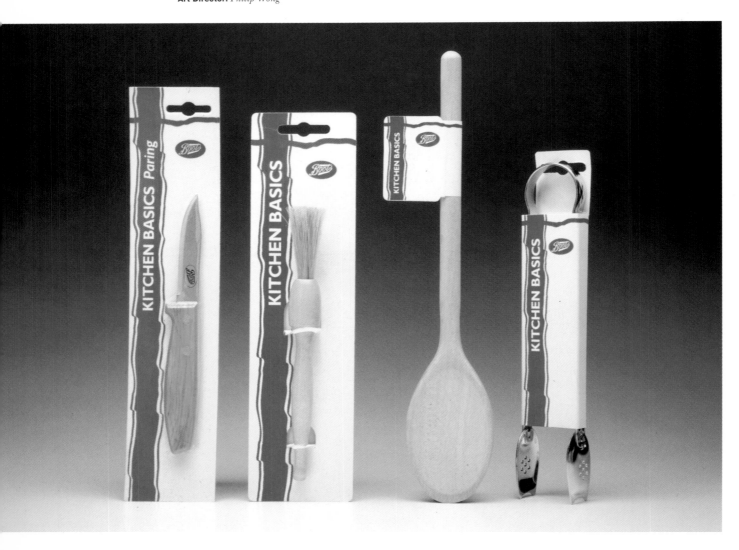

● **Carter Wong**

Originally the packaging designs
for these and the professional
kitchenware products opposite were
very similar to one another.

Boots' brief to Carter Wong was to
create a system which would clearly
differentiate the basic and professional ranges from each other, and
one which would work across a
diverse range of products which included items such as a potato peeler
and a pestle and mortar.

The designs also had to be striking
enough to stand out on the store
shelf.

Carter Wong's solution was to use
simple culinary imagery: the red
stripe of a traditional tea towel for
the basic range and the classic dark
navy blue and white stripe of a chef's
apron for the professional range.

As well as working across the client's
existing product range, this solution
is sufficiently flexible to be able to
accommodate any future products
Boots may introduce.

PROFESSIONAL *Pestle & Mortar*

Boots

Carter Wong

The packaging for this range of professional kitchenware was re-designed by Carter Wong in parallel with their work on Boots' basic product range.

Their simple navy blue and white stripe motif reflects the colours in a chef's apron, just as the red stripe of a traditional tea towel is used in the designs for the basic range.

In both cases the design system is sufficiently flexible to allow for new products to be introduced at any time.

• *Projecting a professional style for The Boots Company plc*
Designers: *Alison Tomlin and Philip Wong*
Art Director: *Philip Wong*
Illustrator: *John Lawrence*

● Davies Hall

This is one of those occasions when simple ideas - which are often the best - actually work.

Davies Hall's identity for Tesco's range of baking tins uses a strong graphic device to link together a wide variety of tins of different shapes and sizes. The leaping gingerbread man is used not only as a symbol of baking, but also suggests the non-stick quality of the product.

The fun of this friendly approach sets Tesco's range apart from its more hard-edged competitors.

● *A friendly face for Tesco's baking tins*
Designer: *Steve Davies*
Art Director: *Steve Davies*
Illustrator: *George Hardie*

● *Fresh ideas for Boots*
Cookware range
Designer: *Adrian McKay*
Art Director: *Alan Colville*
Photographer: *Clive White*

● **Ian Logan Design**

As part of a plan to bring a whole new look to Boots extremely successful Kitchen Department, the designers were briefed to produce packaging for the saucepans, coffee pots, woks and other items which make up Boots Cookware range.

Through innovative photography and styling, the designers produced a range of packs which the client regards as fresh and highly successful.

Pemberton & Whitefoord

In a sector dominated by several major and specialist brands, the cohesive design theme of special wood finishes adopted by Tesco creates an own brand range which has strong shelf impact and a well defined personality.

The marquetry images - each one denoting a particular fragrance or selection of ingredients - endorse many traditional values associated with caring for furniture and family possessions. They also promote the products' inherent quality, and highlight environmental issues such as their ozone friendly nature and the fact they were not tested on animals.

The colour coded caps make for a clear distinction between the three polish types, and help customers make the right selection.

● *Traditional values for
Tesco Stores' furniture polish*
Designer: *Adrian Whitefoord*
Art Directors: *Simon Pemberton
and Adrian Whitefoord*
Illustrator: *Julia Barrett*

A sharp design for Woolworths plc
Designer: *Philip Carter*
Art Director: *Philip Carter*
Illustrators: *Jonathan Mercer and Philip Carter*

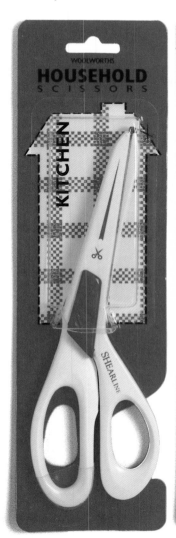

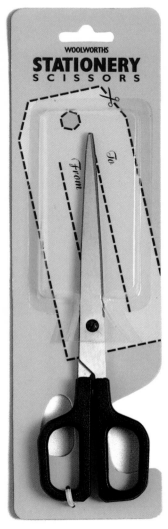
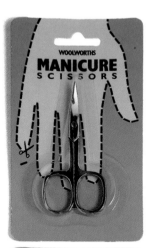

● **Carter Wong**

How to make everyday objects come to life is the problem faced by many packaging designers. Here Carter Wong were given a simple pair of scissors and asked to invest them with an immediate presence in any branch of Woolworths.

Their solution is arresting as well as relevant, and works quickly in the store. The dotted line "cut out" conveys immediately what the product is for; the overall style creates a bright personality for what is a familiar and functional product.

*New designs for dog biscuit
treats for J Sainsbury plc*
Designer: *Yasmin Betteridge*
Art Director: *Richard Ward*
Illustrator: *Patrick Oxenham*

● The Team

The design brief for Sainsbury's range of dog biscuits called for a solution which would increase their sales in competition with other existing brands.

This was achieved through the use of an illustration of a happy, healthy dog in a natural environment. The subtle colouring of the illustration and the evocative subject matter was well received by dog owners who responded favourably to romantic images of their favourite pets.

Both the dog biscuits and the marrowbone rolls have been re-launched as ideal products for today's health conscious market. As well as emphasising their nutritional qualities, the pack designs also project the idea that these products are not just complementary feeding but also a treat.

● *New designs for*
Asda Stores' pet foods
Designer: *Glyn West*
Art Director: *Glyn West*
Illustrator: *Graham Austin*

● **Nettle Design Limited**

The market for canned food for cats and dogs is worth over £850m in the UK, and is dominated by a few major brands such as Whiskas and Pedigree Chum. Own label supermarket penetration is small, although all the major multiples market their own products.

Asda have re-launched their premium brands of cat and dog foods with new names: Tiger and Patch respectively. The new designs feature the kind of strong branding not usually associated with own label products, and illustrations which have proved in research to have a high level of emotional appeal for pet owners.

Since the re-launch, sales have increased by over 50%.

● *A new look for the garden*
at Asda Stores Limited
Designer: *Steve Oxley*
Art Director: *Steve Oxley*
Illustrator: *Steve Oxley*

● Barker Oxley & Cook Partnership

Barker Oxley & Cook was commissioned by Asda to develop
a design capable of bringing together
a range of over 100 separate garden-
related items.

While it was important to create a
cohesive identity for the whole range,
each product had to clearly communicate its own particular function.
Each also had a different packaging
format, which meant that the design
solution had to be flexible enough

to allow it to cater for a wide variety
of formats and a number of different
printing process.

The new design uses a rich shade
of green as a background colour for
each product and a consistent illustrative style to pull the range together. Individual illustrations help
differentiate each product; simple
typography makes the product
information clear and easy to read.

The net result is a range which
appeals to both the enthusiastic
amateur and the skilled expert alike.

*Bringing a new bloom
to Sainsbury's bulbs*
Designer: *Yasmin Betteridge
and Mark Welland*
Art Director: *Richard Ward*

The Team

The brief here was to design a range of packaging for herbaceous bulbs which were to be introduced into the plant sections of Sainsbury's supermarkets.

Using transparencies supplied by the client, the designers created a family of packs which bring a splash of colour to the sales counter.

• *Fresh ideas for Sainsbury's*
Spring Flowering Bulbs
Designers: *Nicole Clément-Weiss*
and Mark Welland
Art Director: *Richard Ward*

• The Team

After a successful trial of a limited range of bulbs in twenty-five stores, Sainsbury's decided to launch a full range of twenty-one lines incorporating new clip-together pvc containers with insert cards.

The brief for this project called for a design with "impulse purchase appeal", hence the use of high impact photography showing the customers exactly what they were going to buy.

A co-ordinated look was also required, to give the range a clear identity and encourage sales of more than one unit. Simple, informative symbols were also introduced giving clear instructions for the bulbs' use, planting, care and so on.

● *Cut flower designs for*
Marks & Spencer
Designer: *Brian Delaney*
Art Director: *Brian Delaney*
Photographer: *Frederique le Fort*

St Michael

Cut flowers

● **Delaney Design Consultants**

The introduction of Marks &
Spencer's range of cut flowers
to be sold in cellophane wrapping
called for a label for the packaging,
as well as design work for the point
of sale material.
  Finding the solution to the problem
was the easy part.
  Finding the correct shape of tulip
bloom proved to be more difficult!

● Trickett & Webb Limited

Trickett & Webb have been retained by Dorma Furnishings for many years now, producing literature such as the company's catalogue, and packaging designs for their wide range of bedlinen, bathroom and kitchenware, as well as for their occasional cosmetic and stationery lines.

The Art of Living range brought Dorma downstairs from upstairs, and introduced the public to a new coordinated collection of furniture, fabrics, curtains and carpets for the living room.

The designers' brief was for a range of packs and swing tickets which would give a coherent identity to a wide range of products made wider still by the great variety of colour-ways for each item.

The solution is a fine example of imaginative yet disciplined thinking which has created a distinct identity for a disparate range of products.

● *Co-ordinated ideas for*
Dorma's Art of Living range
Designers: *Avril Broadley,*
Lynn Trickett and Brian Webb
Art Directors: *Lynn Trickett*
and Brian Webb

• *Projecting the natural*
qualities of Samahdi's oils
Designer: *Martin Seymour*
Art Director: *Alan Coley*

• **Light & Coley**

In all, Samahdi market a ninety-strong range of natural oils. Their brief to Light & Coley was to create a style of packaging which would be distinctive and impactful yet sufficiently aspirational to command a premium price in the market.

The graphics were developed to give the products a strong presence without detracting from an image which communicates an overall softness and subtlety in sympathy with the nature of the products.

The oils' natural qualities are conveyed through product descriptions and through the brand name. The notion of premium quality is emphasised by the inclusion of gold, both in the typography and the labels' border designs.

● *Hammerite for Hunting*
Specialised Products
Designer: *Mark Thrush*
Art Director: *Mark Wickens*
Photographer: *Dave Gill*

● **Wickens Tutt Southgate**

Hammerite is an unusual product. Research showed that consumers loved it and thought it was unrivalled in terms of its performance. But the old pack design - a simple blue and white logo which looked very specialised - did not reflect this. Neither did it convey what the designers discovered: that Hammerite not only does a good job as a protective paint, but also enhances the surface it is applied to.

So, to symbolise Hammerite's protective qualities and its ability to enhance, a model shield was devised which uses the twisting and curling imagery of wrought iron. This was then painted in a variety of Hammerite colours and photographed to highlight both the hammered and smooth finishes available.

The new design aims to broaden Hammerite's appeal by reflecting the enthusiastic DIYer's pride in a job well done.

SHAVER ADAPTOR
For use with all mains operated shavers

For use with ladies' shavers

For use with men's shavers

British Standard 5733

3 PLUG ADAPTOR
Fused to prevent accidental overload

Easy fuse access

Insulated pins

13 AMP FUSE

British Standard 5733

POWER CUT ALARM
Warns if power fails

For use with Freezers and other appliances

Audible Warning

Wires as 13 amp plug

British Standard 3456: 101

5 METRE CURLY EXTENSION LEAD
With fused plug

For extra convenience around the home

FUSED 5 amps MAXIMUM LEAD Capacity 1200 watts

5 AMP FUSE

British Standard 6500

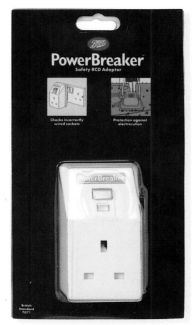

PowerBreaker™
Safety RCD Adaptor

Checks incorrectly wired sockets

Protection against electrocution

British Standard 7071

● *Plugs, adaptors and other*
electrical accessories for Boots
Designer: *Adrian McKay*
Art Director: *Alan Colville*
Illustrator: *Terry Pottle*

● **Ian Logan Design**

As part of the revaluation of their product line, Boots asked Ian Logan Design to look at their full range of electrical packaging.

These products obviously have to project safety as their prime message, as well as show their quality in a visually exciting package.

The design solution is both informative and has a strong visual impact in Boots' stores.

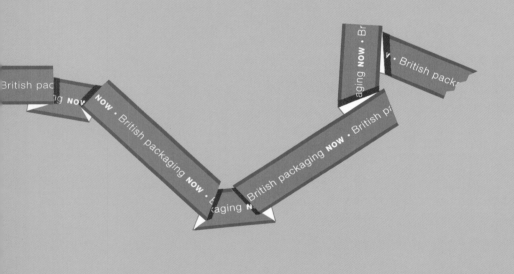

● **Footwear and Clothing**

This section features work commissioned by companies involved in footwear, hosiery, lingerie and sportswear marketing, as well as creative work for an international fashion house.

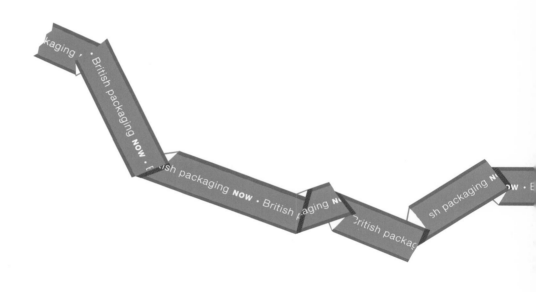

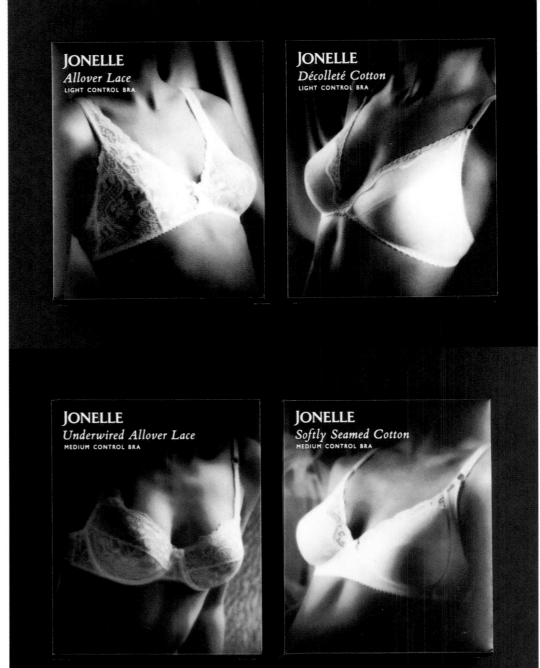

• **Lewis Moberly**

Generally speaking, the major brands in this category adopt white and pastel shades for their pack designs.

The brief for Jonelle bras was to create a new identity for a cohesive range of underwear, clearly denoting the three Light, Medium and Firm product groupings.

The quality and femininity of these products is underscored by the use of softly lit photographs which allow the models to remain anonymous, and thus make it easier for consumers to identity with them. The simple colour coding of the duotone images denotes the strength of each bra and avoids an overclutterd image.

• *Underwear for the*
John Lewis Partnership
Designer: *Lucilla Scrimgeour*
Art Director: *Mary Lewis*
Photographer: *Steve Bicknell*

Boots' hosiery range
Designers: *David Booth*
and Mary Lewis
Art Director: *Mary Lewis*
Illustrator: *Lucilla Scrimgeour*

● **Lewis Moberly**

The re-launch of Boots' own label hosiery followed research which highlighted the problems faced by shoppers trying to chose the right brand. Too often they select the wrong item as the majority of packs fail to communicate vital information such as denier or colour. In trying to solve this problem, most brands have sacrificed their emotional appeal and their brand values, leaving consumers with little or no reason for choosing one brand in preference to another.

Lewis Moberly's design objective was to balance clearly understandable product information with the emotional reward women want from a personal feminine product. Because being able to see the product is important, most packs sport a "bolt on" window as a kind of afterthought to their graphic ideas.

The windows on the Boots range have become the heroes of the packs, in each case showing the product where a woman most wants to see it: on her legs. The strong, simple poses adopted by the models look powerful in mass displays. Bright colour coding is used against the black, white and cream back-grounds to highlight the all important denier and avoid competing with the subtle colours of the products.

● *New designs for Aristoc's*
  two hosiery markets
  Designer: *Rachel Huggett*
  Art Director: *Glyn West*
  Photographer: *Mike Davis*

● **Nettle Design Limited**

Aristoc, which is part of the Coutaulds Group, produce a wide range of fashion hosiery, including a number of brand leaders.

To cater for the increasing demand for fashionable tights which also offer extra support and comfort for the younger end of the market, the company has launched "Vitality".

Two pack formats were designed: one for the traditional department store and hosiery outlets, and another for the increasingly important grocery and multiple chain sector.

Both formats feature strong photographic images depicting the particular lifestyle the product is intended for.

● *A simple solution for*
socks from Tesco's
Designer: *Chen Tsoi*
Art Director: *Chen Tsoi*
Illustrator: *Chen Tsoi*

● **Chen Tsoi Design**

When Tesco decided to re-package their range of ladies' socks, their brief was for a labelling device which would be distinctive yet versatile enough to work across their wide range of styles, colours and patterns.

The simple solution is a typographic one, with an equally simple line drawing working both with and as part of the main type.

Clarks Shoes

This in-house brief called for packaging and point-of-sale material for a new range of children's rugged outdoor shoes.

A sub-brand, Rangers, was created, a symbol designed and then used on the product, its packaging and point-of-sale items.

The look of the design is closely related to the traditional design of jeans labelling, and has been very well received. The packaging has also worked well at the point of sale, which was an important part of the original plan.

Rugged designs for new kids' shoes from Clarks
Designer: *Ian Wills*
Illustrator: *Nigel Lee*

*Soap powder styling for
Clarks' washable shoes*
Designer: *Ian Wills*
Illustrator: *Barrie Dix*

Clarks Shoes

The brief for this project was simple. The shoes are washable so what was wanted was something which would communicate this fact quickly.

The shoe box was designed to look like a washing powder box, with all the copy and illustrations drawn in that style.

The main problem was that the box was printed in the Far East, so that it was impossible to control the final colour values.

However, the result does meet the original objectives, and has done well in the shops.

● *Classic design for*
Fred Perry Sportswear
Designers: *Graham Purnell*
and Ian Prevett
Art Director: *Brian Delaney*

● **Delaney Design Consultants**

The brief for this project was for the design of a gift pack for two shirts, both of which had to be visible within the pack itself.

The objective was to reposition the product within the market, in order to help it compete with more fashionable brands.

The solution involved the design of a clear PVC and cardboard pack with graphics printed onto the cardboard and then bonded to the PVC. The designers' very classic approach relies heavily in the subtle use of the well-known Fred Perry logo.

● *New designs for Joyce Ma*
and her shops
Designers: *Teresa Roviras*
and Stephanie Nash
Art Directors: *Anthony Michael*
and Stephanie Nash
Photographer: *Matthew Donaldson*

● **Michael Nash Associates**

Joyce Ma has a growing number of clothing and lifestyle shops centred in the thriving and challenging retail world of Hong Kong.

Her brief to Michael Nash Associates was for a new brand identity which would work across all her outlets, some of which sell womenswear and menswear by designers such as Dolce & Gabanna, Romeo Gigli, Donna Karan and Issey Miyake.

The work had to be ready in time for the opening of a new clothing and lifestyle shop - which included a flower shop, cafe and homeware section - at the Galleria. Moreover, the designs had to reflect the strong "Joyce" aesthetic and yet still respect several local taboos about the use of certain colours and emblems.

The design is centred on a series of dramatic black and white photographs of flowers and other natural elements which provide a strong recognisable graphic image and a feeling of contemporary purity and elegance, without sacrificing an ability to move with the times as they change.

Michael Nash Associates

This work continues the Joyce Ma design programme in Hong Kong with colour schemes and gift boxes.

● *The Joyce Ma theme continues*
in Hong Kong
Designers: *Teresa Roviras*
and Stephanie Nash
Art Directors: *Anthony Michael*
and Stephanie Nash
Photographer: *Matthew Donaldson*

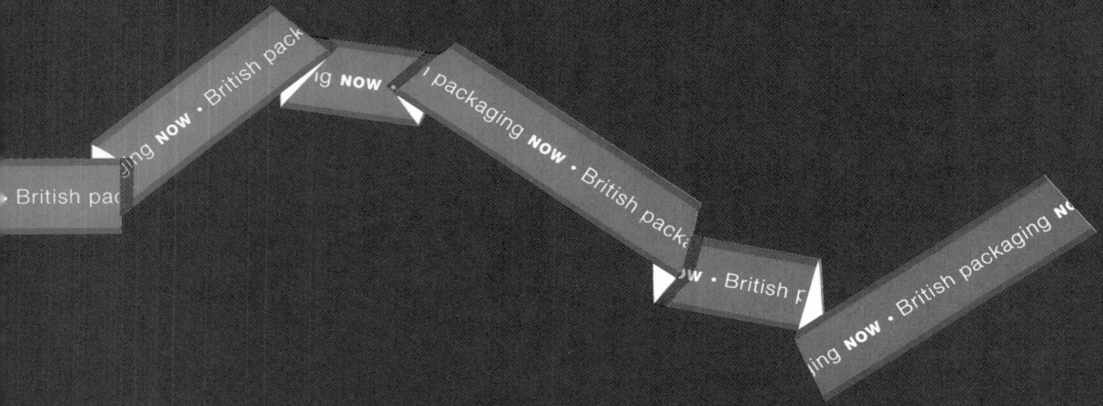

British packaging NOW • British packaging NOW • British packaging NOW • British packaging NOW • British packaging NOW • British packaging NO

Effective packaging can make the difference in any market. This section includes imaginative packaging design for cameras, an engine oil, kites, a Christmas promotional theme and many other products.

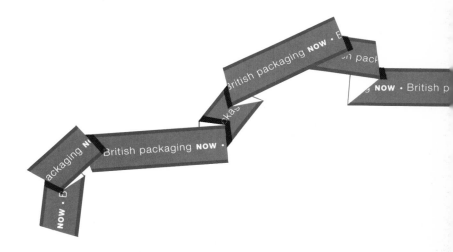

● Walker Izard Limited

Walker Izard was asked to name and design a new brand identity for a range of quality presentation materials from West Design Products. The products are aimed at users of high technology copying equipment such as laser printers and copiers.

The designers conceived an image appropriate for a craft-based product - but which, more importantly, indicated perfection - by using a hand with a finger and thumb just touching.

On each product a hand is holding a different symbolic object. For white presentation paper it holds a delicate china tea cup representing the quality of the hard, shiny paper in the pack. For crystal-clear film the hand holds a diamond. The clear film for colour copiers is represented by a prism.

The brightly coloured labels were used to seal standard white boxes and board envelopes, giving added value to the product while creating an attractive and strongly identifiable range.

● *Reflecting craft and perfection for West Design Products*
Designers: *Cassandra Kingston and Paul Izard*
Art Directors: *Tim Walker and Paul Izard*
Illustrator: *Paul Cox*

● *Re-packaging the Omnicrom*
  range of art materials
Designer: *Mike Staniford*
Art Director: *Mike Staniford*
Illustrator: *Ted Hammond*

● **Hutton Staniford**

Omnicrom products are specifically made for designers and people working in art studios. The products are paper or film-based, and are used in the creation of colour visuals and mock-ups from black and white photocopies.

Letraset acquired the Omnicrom Company and briefed Hutton Staniford to re-package both the existing range of products and some new ones. For reasons of economy, a two-colour design was adopted. The designers were also asked to strengthen the Omnicrom brand name and give a clear identity to each of the various products in the range.

A completely new system of colour coding was introduced, to distinguish the many different products from one another, and to create impact of the point of sale in the busy environment of a graphic art supplies shop. Each of the designs features a pictogram which explains the product's use.

*Respect for the heritage
at Monotype Typography*
Designers: *Michael Denny,
Chris Bradley and Debbie Osborne*
Art Director: *John Bateson*
Photographer: *Gary Tooth*

● Roundel Design Group

Roundel Design were comm-
issioned to create a promotional house style for Monotype
Typography, one of the oldest and
most respected designers and
producers of typefaces in the world.

With the increasing use and
sophistication of desk-top publishing
systems, Monotype are making their
typefaces and supporting products
available on floppy disk and CD
ROM. The house-style devised by
Roundel encompasses font packaging, font catalogues and supporting literature.

The designs respect Monotype's
excellent typographic heritage yet
present the products in a
contemporary and aspirational way.
The font packaging is colour coded
to allow for growth and flexibility
in an expanding portfolio of new
products. The individual packs
contain related literature, including
font index catalogues and user
instruction manuals.

● *WH Smith's Technocrat range*
Designer: *Neil Walker*
Art Director: *Mike Dempsey*
Photographer: *Andy Seymour*

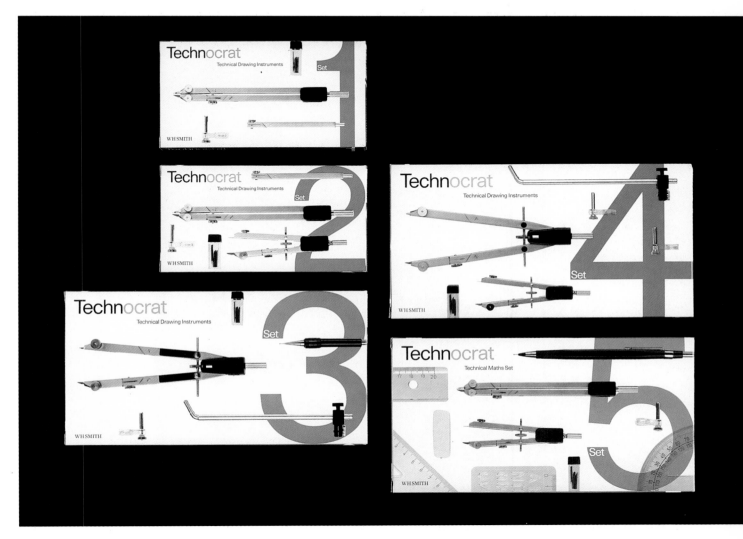

● **Carroll Dempsey & Thirkell**

W H Smith's challenging brief for this project called for packaging for its Technocrat range of drawing instruments which would show all the contents of each of the sets full size and emphasise the high quality and precision tooling of the instruments.

The designers' inspiration came from the form and function of the instruments themselves. The clean, crisp typography and the geometric nature of the layout together with the large identifying numerals give a clear and definite purpose to each of the sets.

● *A multiple image for*
Nikon UK's F-401X
Designer: *David Wood*
Art Director: *Marc Jones*
Photography: *Nikon Photography*

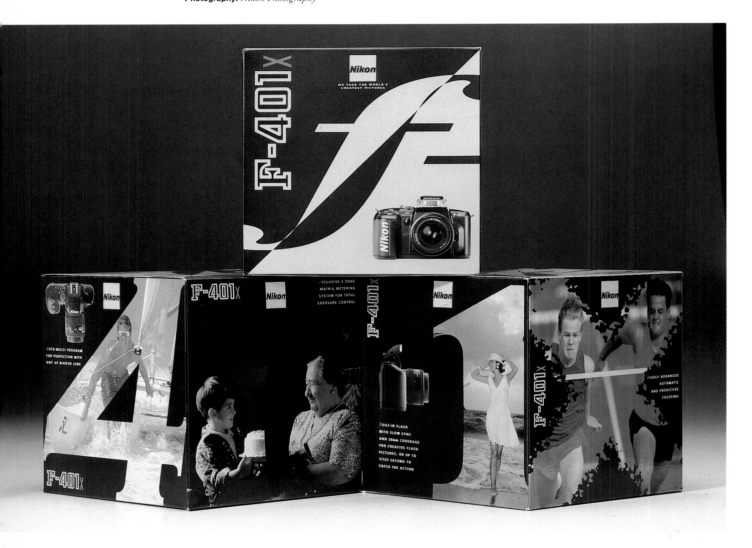

● **Kingsland Lloyd Petersen**

Nikon UK's brief for this project called for a highly visible pack which would reflect the quality of the company's professional heritage and form the basis of a point-of-sale system.

The design of the display pack shows off the quality and variety of photographic images which can be obtained with the F-401X camera. The product's code name was also incorporated into the design in such a way that, by stacking and arranging the packs in the correct configuration, the design would maximise the name's impact on the shelf.

Additional images on the pack also illustrate some of the F-401X's specific technical features, such as Automatic and Predictive focusing and Five Zone Matrix Metering.

● *Snappy packaging for Nikon*
UK's All Weather AW35
Designer: *Louisa Britton*
Art Director: *Marc Jones*

● **Kingsland Lloyd Petersen**

Nikon UK's brief for the packaging for the All Weather AW35 called for a design solution which would be both stylish and recognisably from the house of Nikon, and communicate the idea that this waterproof, action-orientated camera is a piece of fun-to-use technical wizardry.

The design employs clean, simple illustrations, stylised typography, three-colour printing and a cut-out with an acetate sheet which highlights the camera's waterproof qualities.

The whole effect projects an image of technology harnessed to capture fun.

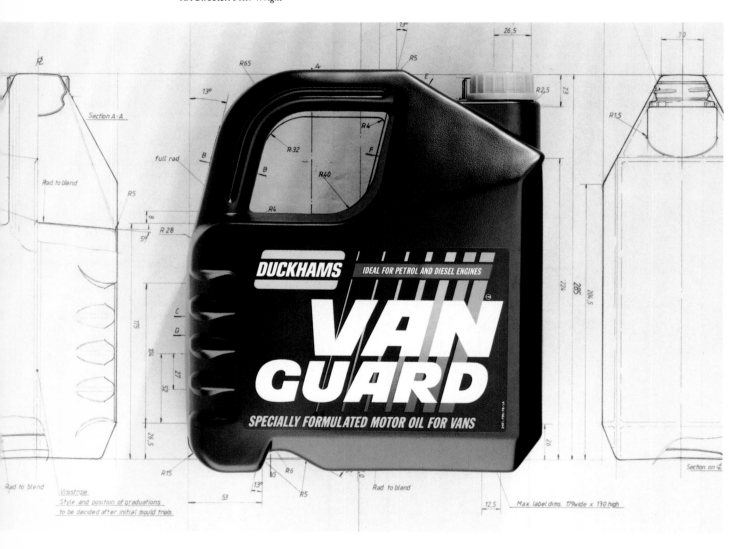

New designs for a niche market
for Alexander Duckham & Co
Designer: *Peter Wright*
Art Director: *Peter Wright*

Top Associates

Commissioned to design a pack and its surface graphics for a niche market, Top Associates saw this project as an ideal opportunity for demonstrating the value of combining pack design with corporate communications.

The result is a strong and consistent message which maximises the visual impact of the product.

The 5 litre can was specifically designed for drivers of small commercial vehicles exposed to a variety of tough working conditions. This called for a broad aesthetic appeal which clearly expressed the functional qualities of the product.

An identity was developed to achieve this by combining the workmanlike characteristics of the name with strong graphics designed to reflect all weather conditions, the details of a tyre tread and a clear understanding of the corporate identity. The brief also required the design to work within parameters dictated by the filling line, which resulted in predetermined dimensions for the pack's "footprint" and its neck height.

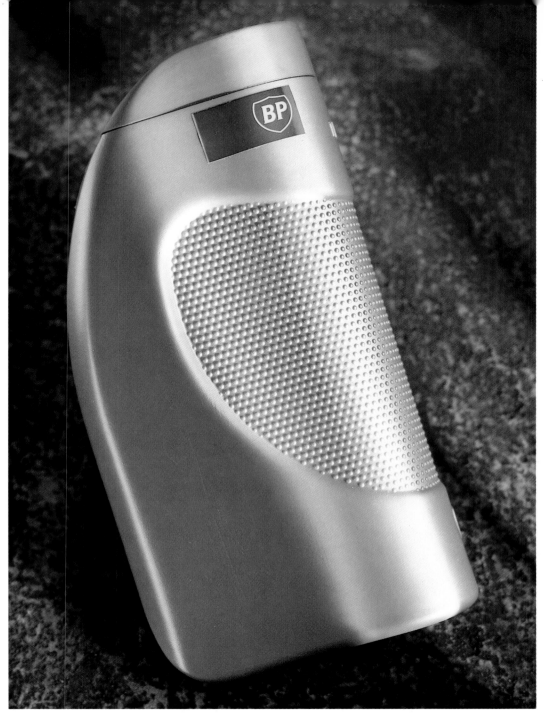

Michael Peters Limited

This revolutionary pack was designed for BP's top-of-the-range VISCO 5000 engine oil.

The designer's main objective was to transform what had previously been a simple can of oil into an elegant, functional structure which would develop into a strong, valuable brand for the company.

The design for the container borrows heavily from the increasingly sophisticated, aerodynamically advanced language of contemporary car design.

The can's handling qualities - its ergonomic design and its smooth-pouring spout hidden beneath a tamper-proof cap - were influenced by current thinking in sports equipment design.

The final appearance, with its silver metallic finish, captures the essence of a well-designed, fast car, and has an instant appeal to the target market of young, sophisticated style-conscious people interested in high performance and aspiring to cars to match.

● Transforming BP's engine
oil market
Designer: Garrick Hamm
Art Director: Glenn Tutssel

Ashted Dastor Associates

The National Gallery's brief to Ashtead Dastor was for a simple protective tube for posters designed to replace the existing one which the Gallery felt looked tired and out-of-date and - they believed - was adversely affecting sales in their shop.

A number of different design concepts were explored before this solution was selected.

Its strong image, which capitalises on the columns at the entrance to the Gallery to create a clever image drawn from the exterior of one of London's most famous landmarks, needs no words to express its functional yet decorative purpose.

In the first twelve months after their introduction, the new tubes were so popular the Gallery shop sold over 20,000 of them as objects in their own right, over and above those they sold as protective cartons for posters and prints.

● *Capitalising on an exterior
feature for The National Gallery*
Designer: *Ashted Dastor*
Art Director: *Ashted Dastor*
Illustrator: *Trevor Lawrence*

- *A special theme for Harrods'*
  Christmas promotion
  Designers: *Marita Lashko,*
  Greg Quinton and Martin Devlin
  Art Director: *Aziz Cami*
  Illustrator: *John Lawrence*

● The Partners

In order to quicken the pace of life in the store, and to create additional marketing opportunities, Harrods runs a number of promotions during the year when the store takes on a different identity for a short period of time. In effect, the store becomes the vehicle for the theme or concept.

The first of these promotions was the Edwardian Christmas theme, expressed through interior design,

displays, packaging, window dressing, catalogues, direct mail and advertising.

The Partners were commissioned to produce the core graphic idea as a catalyst for Harrods' own design team and its public relations and advertising agencies. Due to the sheer size of the store, the theme had to work as a very simple but big brushstroke idea.

An Edwardian engraving of Harrods and Art Nouveau swirls were used for the white label and the boldly striped

background design. The idea of a strong background pattern combined with a label provided a kit of parts for every application.

Agenda Design Associates

Worlds Apart, the largest kite manufacturer in the UK, produces over seventy different types of kite.

Agenda Design were commissioned to carry out a comprehensive packaging audit and then recommend a design rationale for the company's complete product range.

The first packs to be re-designed and re-launched have been grouped together as Worlds Apart's traditional range. Their design has to appeal to a broad customer age group, communicate each product's personality and give each one a dynamic shelf presence.

The designs build on images of family life and the enjoyment of nature and the outdoors. The classic illustrations, rich colours and bold typography create a striking solution full of smiles.

• Traditional kites repackaged
for Worlds Apart Limited
Designer: *Paul Davis*
Art Director: *Paul Davis*
Illustrator: *Lian Findlay*

● *Food packaging and*
carrier bags for Hediard of Paris
Designers: *Peter Windett*
and Penelope Parker
Art Director: *Peter Windett*

● Peter Windett & Associates

This packaging was just one part of a project brief for a new, consistent brand identity for the Paris-based luxury food company, Hediard.

The old packaging was considered to be dated, lacked impact on the shelf and differed in style from one product to another. A single logotype and packaging theme was needed, to give both the packages and the company's shops an up-market and consistent image.

Black and red were retained from the existing livery and incorporated into smart, distinctive stripes which could be used easily across a variety of packaging shapes, as well as on shop blinds and interiors. Gold was employed to combine with the red and black to create a look of luxury. The gold logo and its initial form are used consistently across the various product packs, and applied at a slight angle on the carrier bags to suggest a jaunty spontaneity.

Ian Logan Design

The brief for this project was to produce a modern, lively and fun range of packaging which would appeal to children between the ages of 4 and 10.

The designers felt the range should be kept relatively simple by the use of imaginative illustration and primary colours.

The illustrator, Paul Hampson, produced his work for the boxes and, where possible, cut-outs were made to both show the products and create fun packaging.

● *Children's art materials for WH Smith*
Designer: *Adrian McKay*
Art Director: *Alan Colville*
Illustrator: *Paul Hampson*

Ian Logan Design

The brief from WH Smith for this project was to produce a theme across a range of different types of pencil tins and boxes.

The designers used Noah's ark as the theme and briefed the illustrator Jenny Tylden-Wright - who works with pencils - to interpret this.

The design had to emphasise the different techniques which the pencils could produce. The result shows the gradation of colour from one end of the box to the other, as well as showing the ways in which the pencils can be used. Also, as the boxes become smaller, the illustration comes nearer to the ark.

● *A range of pencil tins and boxes for WH Smith*
Designer: *Adrian McKay*
Art Director: *Alan Colville*
Illustrator: *Jenny Tylden-Wright*

Trickett & Webb Limited

W H Smith's concern for well-designed packaging extends to even the most down-to-earth of their products.

This range of felt pens for students and school children comes to Smith's from a wide variety of suppliers.

However, Trickett & Webb's imaginative designs unite them all with the common motif of "pens as something else".

The universally white backgrounds give the colours of the pens and the illustrations a clean background to work against.

The illustrations are rarely relevant, but always witty.

The entire range has an eye-catching character which suggests that all the pens will be fun to use.

● WH Smith's range of
felt pens for children
Designers: *Suzanne Evans,*
Lynn Trickett and Brian Webb
Art Directors: *Lynn Trickett*
and Brian Webb
Illustrator: *Brian Grimwood*

• Bright ideas for bright kids
at WH Smith
Designers: *Suzanne Evans,*
Lynn Trickett and Brian Webb
Art Directors: *Lynn Trickett*
and Brian Webb
Illustrator: *Jason Ford*

● **Trickett & Webb Limited**

WH Smith's Creative Play products were conceived as activity kits to be bought as gifts by adults for children and by children for other children for around £5.

The range includes mask and basket making kits, glove and finger puppet kits and even one which will introduce children to the eighteenth century art of quilling.

The fresh yet slightly cheeky images of children on the packs were deliberately created to give today's children someone sparky to identify with. The flat coloured panels were designed to provide a table-top surface on which the component parts are played with.

The designers chose the drum shaped cartons with the idea that they could be kept and used for storing other things, such as pens or pencils or collections of objects.

The entire range is accompanied by a highly successful selection of accessories such as sequins, gummed paper shapes and coloured pipe cleaners. There is even a pack of wooly bits which would be hard to find anywhere but in Smith's.

● *WH Smith's Recycled*
  Paper Products
  Designer: *Tamara Williams*
  Art Director: *Alan Colville*
  Illustrator: *Beverly Levy*

● **Ian Logan Design**

This lively design emphasises recycling through the use of a crumpled paper image, and the concept of saving trees by the loose illustration of a tree trunk.

The design has proved to be very successful in the stores.

The Partners

As one of the company's four design consultants, one of the first projects undertaken by The Partners for WH Smith was the re-design of their largest own brand range: stationery for the home and office.

The brief was to make the packaging look more engaging through an idea which was flexible enough to cover over three hundred items, ranging from paper clips to envelope packs.

The chosen route features cartoons by Larry, the chronicler of the common man, whose drawings reflect the lives of both the products and their users.

The range is unified by a standard form of label information and a clear colour coding system. The product names are all displayed in scribble typeface.

Market research has shown that customers find the packs attractive, consistent and informative.

● *Cartoon approach for*
WH Smith's stationery range
Designer: *Marita Lashko*
Art Directors: *Aziz Cami*
and David Stuart
Illustrator: *Terence Parks*

● *Putting a lively face on*
Expressions for WH Smith
Designers: *Avril Broadley,*
Lynn Trickett and Brian Webb
Art Directors: *Lynn Trickett*
and Brian Webb

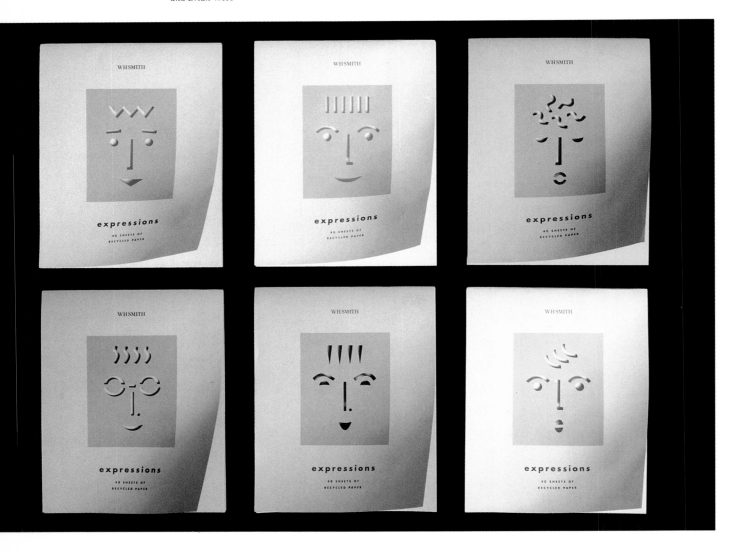

● Trickett & Webb Limited

When WH Smith briefed Trickett & Webb on designs for their Expressions range of recycled paper, the name was already agreed.

As the product is both recycled and self-coloured, the designers wanted to keep their input as low-key as possible, believing that over embellishing the paper would defeat its value as an environmentally conscious product.

The images of facial expressions are a simple, witty pun on both the product name and the self-expression embodied in personal letter writing.

In the larger scheme of things, even the scraps of paper left over from the die cutting are recycled.

Trickett & Webb Limited

This range of recycled stationery - which is less expensive than Expressions - was designed for WH Smith's younger customers. Its simplicity, and its amusing image has proved very successful. The designers' attention to detail can be seen in the way the paper sizes and numbers of sheets of paper or envelopes in a pack are cleverly displayed within the pastiche of a postmark.

WH Smith's recycled paper
for the youth market
Designers: *Andy Thomas,*
Lynn Trickett and Brian Webb
Art Directors: *Lynn Trickett*
and Brian Webb

● *WH Smith's Camomile Stationery Set*
Designer: *Nicola Chapman*
Art Director: *Alan Colville*

● Ian Logan Design

This brief called for a range of stationery which would have the feel of "home made" or "craft made" products. It also had to appeal to a market which buys pot pourri and dried flowers.

The designers decided to employ a small craft paper making company, and use real flowers and plants for photography. The paper company produced an A3 sheet of hand-made paper which was photographed and used throughout the range.

These products are sold alongside WH Smith's recycled papers and their very successful "Flora Bundi" stationery range.

● *One of WH Smith's special*
stationery ranges for the
gift market
Designers: *Sarah Mattinson,*
Lynn Trickett and Brian Webb
Art Directors: *Lynn Trickett*
and Brian Webb
Photographer: *Carol Sharp*

● **Trickett & Webb Limited**

Launched in time for Christmas 1992, Orchard is just one of the special stationery ranges WH Smith produce for the gift market.

The entire range includes not only writing paper and envelopes, but note books, address books, jotter pads and boxed sets which double as letter racks when the paper and envelopes have been used up.

The photographic image which binds the range together is evocative of late summer fruits and is a complete departure from the fabric-based images used on earlier products of this kind. Cleverly used, it wraps round some items like a patterned skin, giving the various items a strong collective identity.

● **Trickett & Webb Limited**

Faced with the problem of how to make WH Smith's assorted Christmas cards yet more attractive, Trickett & Webb decided to gift-wrap the cards themselves.

These two packs were created by producing classically-styled wrapping paper and photographing it in conjunction with simple ribbons tied in bows. The resulting images were then printed onto standard cartons and embellished with seasonal graphics.

The final packages are attractive both as containers for the cards and gift boxes in their own right.

Trickett & Webb Limited

Having wrapped WH Smith's classic Christmas cards in richly coloured boxes decorated with predominantly green and red paper, Trickett & Webb's design for their client's recycled cards seems almost obvious.

It is the "grunge" version of the same idea.

Where the original papers were heavy with colour, the recycled cards are boxed in plain brown paper. Ribbon has been replaced with string and sealing wax, and the price is displayed as a simple rubber stamped image.

The whole effect is perfectly suited to the green issue and the practicalities of recycling.

A recycled image for WH Smith's recycled Christmas cards
Designers: *Andy Thomas, Lynn Trickett and Brian Webb*
Art Directors: *Lynn Trickett and Brian Webb*
Photographer: *Carol Sharp*

● *A strong design for WH Smith's*
illuminated globe
Designers: *Suzanne Evans,*
Lynn Trickett and Brian Webb
Art Directors: *Lynn Trickett*
and Brian Webb
Photographer: *Peter Marshall*

● Trickett & Webb Limited

As well as marketing a massive range of stationery and related products, WH Smith has a substantial share of the educational equipment market. Their range of globes - which includes an inflatable one - is one example.

The problem facing Trickett & Webb in this particular instance was how to demonstrate how this product worked. The surface design of the globe shows the political, geographical and topographical detail of the whole world. When it is illuminated it shows the political detail. When it is not it shows the topographical detail.

The solution comes from two photographs carefully butted together to show the two faces of the world side by side and at the same time.

The image also includes the cable and switch, to indicate how the globe works.

Part of the brief also called for designs which would stand being stacked on shop floors, rather than on shelves. The strong typographic styling ensures that the packs will not be lost in the hurly burly of a High Street store.

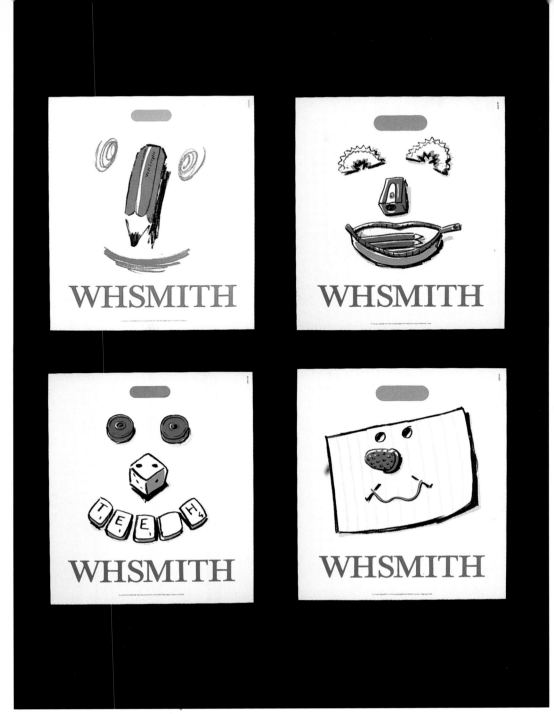

As the largest retailers of stationery, books and magazines in the country, WH Smith were faced with the challenge of how to make their carrier bags more visible on High Streets up and down the country. In 1991 they asked The Partners to create designs for a new carrier bag range.

After studying the company's retail operation in detail, The Partners recommended that the new bags should be used to convey a selling message about the vast product range on offer in WH Smith's branches.

The solution uses the company's products to make up a series of friendly "product" faces.

• *A friendly face for*
WH Smith's carrier bags
Designer: *James Beveridge*
Art Directors: *James Beveridge*
and David Stuart
Illustrator: *Geoff Appleton*

Hutton Staniford Limited,
5 Apollo Studios,
Charlton Kings Road,
London NW5 2SB
Tel: 071 482 2140 Fax 071 485 6068
Contact: Mike Staniford
p.41, 49, 227

Darrell Ireland,
The Foundry,
27 Hoxton Street,
London N1 6NH
Tel: 071 739 4512 Fax: 071 229 7278
Contact: Darrell Ireland
p.118, 119, 129, 149, 155

The Jenkins Group,
9 Tufton Street,
London SW1P 3QB
Tel: 071 799 1090 Fax: 071 222 6751
Contact: Deborah Boustead
p.81

Jones Knowles Ritchie,
Second Floor,
79 Parkway,
London NW1 7PP
Tel: 071 284 3878 Fax: 071 284 3879
Contact: Jonathan Kirk
p.62, 154

KLP Partners Limited,
The Old Chapel,
Fairview Drive,
Redland,
Bristol BS6 6PW
Tel: 0272 420388 Fax: 0272 420770
Contact: Stewart Macdonald
p.230, 231

Kyte & Company Limited,
11-12 Whitehorse Mews,
Westminster Bridge Road,
London SE1 7QD
Tel: 071 620 0828 Fax: 071 401 2403
Contact: Ray Kyte
p.19, 23, 33, 40, 58, 141

Lewis Moberly,
33 Gresse Street,
London W1P 1PN
Tel: 071 580 9252 Fax: 071 255 1671
Contact: Mary Lewis
*p.15, 17, 32, 48, 67, 76, 126, 127, 153,
168, 174, 178, 214, 215*

Light & Coley Limited,
20 Fulham Broadway,
London SW6 1AH
Tel: 071 381 6644 Fax: 071 381 2833
Contact: Alan Coley
p.146, 160, 163, 209

Raymond Loewy International,
25/30 Plympton Street,
London NW8 8AB
Tel: 071 402 8601 Fax: 071 724 7216
Contact: Thomas Riedel
p.161

Ian Logan Design Company,
42 Charterhouse Square,
London EC1M 6EU
Tel: 071 606 1803 Fax: 071 726 6419
Contact: Ian Logan or Gail Moss
p.64, 66, 199, 211, 238, 239, 242, 246

The London Design Partnership,
The Works,
Torriano Mews,
London NW5 2RZ
Tel: 071 485 5885 Fax: 071 267 3115
Contact: Gerard O'Dwyer
p.63, 90, 91, 133, 158, 166, 175

McIlroy Coates Limited,
10 Bernard Street,
Leith,
Edinburgh EH6 6PP
Tel: 031 555 1342 Fax: 031 555 1343
Contact: Lynn Hall
p.10, 120

Miller Sutherland,
6 D'Arblay Street,
London W1V 3FD
Tel: 071 437 2901 Fax: 071 734 6028
Contact: Siân Sutherland
or Kathy Miller
p.52, 93, 101, 109, 170, 171

**Minale Tatttersfield & Partners
Limited,**
The Courtyard,
37 Sheen Road,
Richmond,
Surrey TW9 1AJ
Tel: 081 948 7999 Fax: 081 948 2435
Contact: Liza Honey
*p.16, 43, 72, 79, 106, 107, 111, 177,
182, 186*

Michael Nash Associates,
42-44 Newman Street,
London W1P 3PA
Tel: 071 631 3370 Fax: 071 637 9629
Contact: Wendy Gilliatt
p.221, 222, 223

Nettle Design Limited,
'O' Warehouse,
Metropolitan Wharf,
Wapping Wall,
London E1 9SS
Tel: 071 265 0957 Fax: 071 702 0506
Contact: John Hurst
p.18, 22, 27, 74, 85, 99, 121, 203, 216

The Partners,
Albion Courtyard,
Greenhill Rents,
London EC1M 6BN
Tel: 071 608 0051
Fax: 071 250 0473/3917
Contact: David Stuart
p.190, 235, 243, 251

Pemberton & Whitefoord,
52 Gloucester Place,
London W1H 3HJ
Tel: 071 486 0827 Fax: 071 486 1899
Contact: Simon Pemberton
p.110, 200

Pentagram Design Limited,
11 Needham Road,
London W11 2RP
Tel: 071 229 3477 Fax: 071 727 9932
Contact: Deborah Richardson
p.56, 169

Michael Peters Limited,
49 Princes Place,
London W11 4QA
Tel: 071 229 3424 Fax: 071 221 7720
Contact: Jonathan Davis
*p.21, 34, 55, 75, 86, 134, 136, 137,
138, 143, 156, 157, 193, 194, 195, 233*

Tor Pettersen & Partners Limited,
56 Greek Street,
London W1V 5LR
Tel: 071 439 6463 Fax: 071 434 1299
Contact: Tor Pettersen
p.183

Roundel Design Group,
7 Rosehart Mews,
Westbourne Grove
London W11 3TY
Tel: 071 221 1951 Fax: 071 221 1843
Contact: Charlotte Lawrie
p.228

Saatchi & Saatchi Design,
80 Charlotte Street,
London W1A 1AQ
Tel: 071 636 5060 Fax: 071 436 8923
Contact: Geogina Urwin
p.102

Shiel Humphrey Design,
1 Northfields Prospects,
Putney Bridge Road,
London SW18 1HX
Tel: 081 874 2408 Fax: 081 874 7765
Contact: Patricia Sheil
p.59

David Spencer Design Partnership,
5 Langley Street,
London WC2H 9JA
Tel: 071 836 6892 Fax: 071 240 2202
Contact: David Spencer
p.57

Springett Associates,
13 Salisbury Place,
London W1H 1FJ
Tel: 071 486 7527 Fax: 071 487 3033
Contact: Rod Springett
p.24, 60, 88

Michael Stewart Design,
21 Church Road,
Poole,
Dorset BH14 8UF
Tel: 0202 715175 Fax: 0202 715130
Contact: Michael Thrasher
p.104

The Team,
The Church Hall,
120 Putney Bridge Road,
London SW15 2NQ
Tel: 081 877 0888 Fax: 081 874 6994
Contact: Richard Ward
p.25, 26, 54, 140, 179, 202, 205, 206

Michael Thierens Design,
49 St. Margaret's Road,
Twickenham,
Middlesex TW1 2LL
Tel: 081 744 2996 Fax: 081 892 1817
Contact: Michael Thierens
p.44, 87, 96, 97

Top Associates,
David Mews,
11A Greenwich South Street,
London SE10 8NW
Tel: 081 305 2788 Fax: 081 858 2128
Contact: Peter Wright
p.232

Trickett & Webb Limited,
The Factory,
84 Marchmont Street,
London WC1N 1AG
Tel: 071 388 5832 Fax: 071 387 4287
Contact: Brian Webb or Lynn Trickett
*p.20, 30, 37, 94, 172, 173, 208, 240,
241, 244, 245, 247, 248, 249, 250*

Turner Duckworth Limited,
Voysey House,
Barley Mow Passage,
London W4 4PH
Tel: 081 994 7190 Fax: 081 994 7192
Contact: Holly Day
or Bruce Duckworth
p.108

Visser Bay Anders Toscani Design,
Assumburg 152,
1081 GC Amsterdam,
Holland
Tel: 31 20 6462566
Fax: 31 20 6462634
Contact: Eugene Bay
p.95, 98, 100

Walker Izard Limited,
35 Homer Street,
London W1H 1HL
Tel: 071 723 9911 Fax: 071 724 0349
Contact: Paul Izard
p.226

Wickens Tutt Southgate,
11 Heathman's Road,
London SW6 4TJ
Tel: 071 384 2316 Fax: 071 731 2003
Contact: Paul Southgate
p.83, 89, 103, 210

Peter Windett & Associates,
55-57 South Edwardes Square,
London W8 6HP
Tel: 071 221 0301 Fax: 071 602 6545
Contact: Peter Windett
p.46, 50, 122, 123, 167, 237

Klaus Wuttke and Partners Limited,
5-6 Clipstone Street,
London W1P 7EB
Tel: 071 323 2721 Fax: 071 255 1562
Contact: Klaus Wuttke
p.176, 187

Ziggurat Design Consultants Limited,
20 Chenies Street,
London WC1E 7EX
Tel: 071 636 9966 Fax: 071 255 1187
Contact: Bernard Gormley
p.132, 144, 145, 150, 162